CONTENT THAT CONVERTS

How To Build A Profitable and Predictable
B2B Content Marketing Strategy

LAURA HANLY

CONTENTS

"Laura has a great ability to draw out the nuances of the way things are done in other people's businesses. Her writing is fantastic and the delivery is spot-on."
— Tristan King, owner of Blackbelt Commerce, highest rated Shopify agency in the world

Laura is a content machine that pumps out excellence onto paper. She took my outline, extracted the information from me, was very responsive and patient, and delivered a final manuscript I was very pleased with. We were an Amazon bestseller in my category and have 95%+ 5 star reviews at this point in time. I would recommend Laura and her team to anyone.
— Jeff Root, owner, SellTermLife & bestselling author of The Digital Life Insurance Agent

"Using your strategies, we're getting more sales and people are much more engaged. Good work!"
— Scott Desgrosseilliers, owner, Wicked Reports

"Can I say again how smoothly this process has gone and how happy I am with the manuscript you developed. I'm so grateful that this whole part of the process was completely taken off my hands. Marketing a book is difficult and tedious enough without the additional burden of drafting the manuscript, and the fact that I'm so proud of the manuscript (much more so than I would have been if I'd written the whole thing myself) gives me the extra motivation to make the launch as successful as the book deserves."
— Kiri Masters, owner, Bobsled Marketing Agency

"I highly recommend Laura if you need help with content marketing strategy. Mind blown."
— Coran Woodmass, owner, The FBA Seller

"It's immediately apparent what a seasoned expert Laura is in her field. She provides great insights and lays out a clear direction for content strategy."
— Jay Schaefer, owner, Adego Marketing

"Laura, I am so blown away by your work. It is SO GOOD! Thank you for listening to us, creating inspired content, and encouraging and enabling us to hone in on our message and story. It's remarkable what you've been able to bring to our team."
— Sadie Roberts, owners, Tradlands

"Laura did a quick and thorough analysis of our website and sales process and was able to come up with some great ways to improve our user experience and increase our conversion optimization through a number of email marketing strategies."
— Ravi Coutinho, World Wide Golf Adventures

Chapter One: Developing Your Content Marketing Strategy

Content marketing is a powerful arm to add to your overall marketing strategy. It establishes you as an authority, it increases your revenue, and has high profit potential. Bill Gates talked about this way back in 1996, as the Internet was starting to come into its own:

"Content is where I expect much of the real money will be made on the Internet, just as it was in broadcasting... The broad opportunities for most companies involve supplying information or entertainment. No company is too small to participate. One of the exciting things about the Internet is that anyone with a PC and a modem can publish whatever content they can create. In a sense, the Internet is the multimedia equivalent of the photocopier. It allows material to be duplicated at low cost, no matter the size of the audience.

The Internet also allows information to be distributed worldwide at basically zero marginal cost to the publisher. Opportunities are remarkable, and many companies are laying plans to create content for the Internet... [But] if people are to be expected to put up with turning on a computer to read a screen, they must be rewarded with deep and extremely up-to-date information that they can explore at will... They need an opportunity for personal involvement that goes far beyond that offered through the letters-to-the-editor pages of print magazines." [1]

Content is not, however, a magic bullet. It is not a rapid growth strategy, often taking months to grow into its potential. It does not guarantee you internet

---

[1] http://www.craigbailey.net/content-is-king-by-bill-gates/

celebrity, or riches beyond your wildest dreams. (In the wrong hands, it can even harm your brand and put off potential customers, and we'll cover what *not* to do at the end of this chapter.)

Many businesses blog, or podcast, or post on social media for years and never see a dime in return for all their efforts. They might argue that they've built great brand equity, and that they've gained authority and credibility in their industry without selling out. Well, that might be true, but you can't eat brand equity, and you sure as hell can't pay a team with it.

Now, I'm the first to admit that everything would be awesome if I could just write and write and never have to think about whether it was actually going to generate money in return. Unfortunately, that's called going broke — it's not in my 10-year plan, and I'd take a guess that it's not in yours either. The only way to make content marketing pay off is to develop a complete ecosystem around your primary content platform (whether that's your blog, podcast, or YouTube channel), instead of hoping it will just work by itself. Creating a complete system around your content leverages the resources that could help grow your business, instead of wasting them.

For now, understand that every business produces content, whether it's intentional or not. Every business has at least one expert in it. And it's that expertise that provides your business with its competitive edge. You must leverage this as the critical resource in your marketing, so let's dive into how to do that.

To develop any successful marketing strategy, you need to have a clear picture of the goals in your business. This is particularly true of content marketing: sitting down to bang out anything that pops into your head is not a sensible way to approach it. You need to have a consistent strategy for the content you're producing, so that your audience is engaged, comes to know and respect you as an authority, and will buy from you when the time is right. Let's look at how to produce recurring content in a way that will help you achieve those goals *and* keep you motivated to keep producing on a regular basis.

Here are some questions to ask yourself and your team in order to develop a marketing strategy that will serve your business:

- What is the purpose of our marketing?
- Who are we trying to reach?
- What are the types of marketing we should use? Is content the right fit for us?
  - Do we have someone who can produce it?
  - Do we have good ideas about what our content would be focused on?
  - Is our market segment interested in consuming that kind of content?
  - What other kinds of marketing do we need to implement to make our content really perform for us?
- How will we measure success?
- How long is our sales cycle? Can we absorb a delay between implementing this marketing strategy and having it start feeding into the sales cycle?
- What operational adjustments will we need to make as the marketing becomes successful?
- Who will be responsible for each part of the marketing strategy?
- What resources will we need to execute the marketing strategy effectively?

Now, there are two main types of content you can use in a content marketing strategy. There's recurring content, which builds a customer base gradually over time, and there are content assets used as near-term client acquisition tools. But before you commit to either of those options, there are four areas that you need to get very clear on.

I call this the Conversion Quadrant: this is the intersection between your expertise and what your customers want, what you want to be an authority on, how you produce your best content, and your quarterly plan.

1. **What is the intersection between what your customers want and/or need?**

What are the things you really, deeply care about in your business? What are you world class at, and how does that serve your customers? Maybe you believe you have the very best product in your niche and can defend that position. Maybe you go above and beyond for your customers in very tangible ways. Maybe innovation has allowed you to change your industry and is a critical part of how you function. Whatever it might be, brainstorm and explore the things that are most important to you and your business.

Then take a look at your customers: every customer group is different. If you are selling to a fashion niche, maybe your audience takes presentation and style extremely seriously, and want to know what famous stylish people are doing, or what trends they need to be aware of in the coming months. Maybe your audience is very focused on ethical sourcing and production, and want to see transparency and sustainability in the brands they support. What are your customers looking to you for insight about, and how do those topics overlap with the values you outlined above?

2. What do you want to be known as an industry authority for?

A few years ago, Gary Keller and Jay Papasan wrote a book called *The One Thing*. The core idea of that book is to identify the one thing in your business that will make everything else easier or irrelevant… and the same goes for your content marketing. What is the one thing you can focus on becoming known for that will make it easier to develop, market and sell products that your audience will buy again and again?

Gary Vaynerchuk is known for his no-nonsense prioritization of hustle. You know if you work with him that things are absolutely going to get done. Tim Ferriss is known for his endless self-experimentation. You know if you work with him you're going to get innovative, uncommon results. Warren Buffett is known for his slow, measured approach to investing. You know if you work with him that you'll get steady returns over the long term. What is the one thing people should know about working with you?

The simplest way to become an authority on something is to say the same things about that topic over and over again. This is why people like Tony Robbins, Peter Drucker, Charlie Munger and Warren Buffet become superstars in their industries. Firstly, what they say works — it gets the results they claim. But secondly, they hammer on the same things over and over again. They communicate the same messages over the course of their entire careers, and create powerful positioning and profits as a result.

3. What is the format in which you produce your best content?

People will often talk about how you need to tailor your content production to how your audience consumes it. I think it's better to choose the format that you most enjoy working in, because if you like it, your audience will like it. For example: if you're awesome at creating long-form blog posts (like Mark Manson or Tim Urban at Wait But Why) but are lacklustre with video, don't try to wrangle together a YouTube channel.

If you get a kick out of creating the content, it will show: it will engage your audience because it's high energy, it will be focused, and it will address things they care about in a way that shows you care about it too. But if you have to have five espressos and lock yourself in a distraction-free room for a day just to produce one video, the strain and negativity of that is going to come through. This creates a feedback loop: you don't like doing it, so people don't like consuming it, so it doesn't perform. Don't do stuff you hate. If you hate writing, do video. If you hate both, do podcasting. Just find the medium that works for you and run it.

4. What's your quarterly plan?

Last but definitely not least: make a specific plan for the immediate future. Develop content themes to go along with your 'one thing', and map out several topics within each theme to cover over the next three months. Pick four themes total, and three topics per theme. Write the headline for each of the 12 topics, assign a date to each one, and use that as your content framework. You can include any sales campaigns or announcements in this plan if you want to. Simplified, here's the overview of what should be in your quarterly plan:

- A clear statement of your 'one thing'

- Four themes you want to rotate through
- Three topics per theme, including key points to touch on for each
- Headlines for each topic (I recommend brainstorming a few variations so you can pick the best one)
- Scheduled date of publication for each topic

Mapping your content out like this ensures that you can be strategic about your production: you can lead your audience to a certain action over time, you can educate them about a product before you've announced it, or you can just give them a complete, cohesive body of knowledge about the things that you all value. Whatever your goal, creating a plan in advance allows you to use your content to achieve it.

What *Not* To Include In Your Marketing Strategy

Here are a few simple guidelines for what to avoid in your content marketing. These mistakes vary in severity, from annoying to fatal, but all of them are easily avoided. Whenever you're thinking about your content, *remember that the people consuming it are people.* They get distracted and tired. They get offended and hurt. They get excited and motivated. A little empathy goes a long way, particularly if you're referring to specific people in your content. Use this as your North Star and you won't go too far wrong. Here's the cheat sheet:

- Don't try to rip off someone else's style. Find your own voice and positioning — it's obvious when you're just copying what the cool kids are doing.
- Don't bad-mouth your competitors, even when you have an easy shot or would be justified. You'll probably be dealing with them for a very long

time, and it's better to have good or neutral relationships with them rather than slagging them on the internet.

- Don't publish without a plan. Every piece of content that comes out of your business needs to serve a clear, strategic purpose, both for you and your customers.
- Don't try to be all things to all people. If you have a SEO consultancy, you do not need to make your content appealing to people looking for PPC information: focus on what you're good at.
- Don't use your content to spam your audience. Just because it's 'marketing' doesn't mean you can use every post to sell something. Respect your audience and only make offers when it serves them and is strategic for your business.

Don't be complacent. Sloppy work will instantly alienate your audience — 'it'll do' is not good enough. Your content should be pin-sharp or not published.

Action Steps for Chapter One:

1. Create your Conversion Quadrant:
    a. What do you value in your business, what do your customers value, and how do they intersect?
    b. What do you want to be the authority on?
    c. What format of content production works best for you?
    d. What's the quarterly plan for your business, and what kind of content would best support those goals?

Chapter Two: The Content Marketing Ecosystem

Think of a complete content marketing strategy as an ecosystem: content is a dynamic medium, and there are living creatures — your customers — involved in it at every stage, just like a physical ecosystem. Your content strategy will grow and evolve over time, and there have to be a number of elements present for the strategy to be healthy and effective.

There are two types of content ecosystems: recurring systems, and asset systems. A recurring system has six parts that need to be built in for the ecosystem to be healthy; an asset system has four parts. You can use either system on its own in your business, or you can use them both in tandem.

The Six Parts of A Recurring Ecosystem

1. High-quality front end content

This might seem obvious, but everything you publish needs to be great quality: informative, actionable and interesting. It should serve a clear purpose for you *and* your customers. It should be spell-checked and formatted. It should be published on a regular schedule and consistently provide the best information coming out of your industry.

2. An opt-in offer

Your content is going to bring traffic to your site, but that traffic will leave again once it's done with the content. An opt-in offer (usually a pop-up or form on the site that requests an email address in exchange for an asset) captures that traffic, so you can continue marketing to them once they leave your site. Good opt-in offers include white papers, industry reports, educational courses, cheat sheets, checklists, webinars, video courses, coupons or demo/downloads.

3. An email onboarding sequence

Once you've captured a lead with your opt-in offer, you need to onboard them with a sequence of automated emails (which we'll talk about later in the book). A sequence is usually four to eight emails long, and educates the subscriber about your brand, shares some of your best resources, and invites them to connect with you. This engages them on an individual level, increases their investment in your brand and set their expectations for their future interactions with you.

4. An initial conversion opportunity

Once you've nurtured your leads for a while through your email sequence, providing them with lots of valuable information and sharing your expertise generously, it's time to make them an offer. Your interactions prior should have led naturally to this point (by highlighting the benefits that come out of doing business with you), so that the prospect is comfortable with the offer and will be open to taking you up on it.

5. A follow-up sequence

Once you've made your initial offer, you will have two groups: prospects who converted, and those who did not. You need to follow up with both. Those that did convert should a) be offered an upsell or upgrade and b) onboarded to make the most of the product or service they've purchased. Those that did not convert should be a) offered a downsell or 'light' version to try to get a conversion, and b) put into a new sequence that will give further value and education in preparation for the next offer (whether that's the same thing offered in a new way, or an offer of a completely different product or service).

6. Another conversion opportunity (and another, and another...)

Ideally, you'll make multiple offers over the course of your relationship with each customer. It's easier to get a repeat customer than a new one, so you want to build in systems that allow you to maximize the lifetime value of each customer. Whether it's through automated email sequences or launch cycles, you need to have recurring sales systems in place.

The Four Parts of An Asset Ecosystem

1. A high-quality long-form content asset

Content assets include books, web summits, webinar series, or multi-part video courses. For most businesses, books are ideal, because you can use physical copies as real-world calling cards, sending them to potential clients and leveraging them into bigger opportunities for the business (like speaking engagements and interviews).

2. An initial engagement opportunity

This would usually be an invitation for the prospect to get on a call with you, to participate in a webinar or event, or to get a demo of your product. There needs to be a specific next step presented to the prospect once they've engaged with your asset that creates a one-on-one or real-time interaction with you.

3. An initial conversion opportunity

This is as simple as making an offer during the initial engagement. Whether you're on the phone, or talking on a webinar or demo, you should use this moment when you have their undivided attention to invite them to take action on a particular offer.

4. A follow-up email sequence

Again, you will end up with two groups: the prospects that converted, and those that did not. Both groups need follow-up. Your new customers should be onboarded and upsold through one email sequence, your customers-in-waiting should be downsold and put into a different sequence that will make them more amenable to your next offer.

• • •

It's critical that there is a specific guiding principle for all your marketing. This principle or goal should direct all your decisions, make decision-making easier, and keep you focused on the right things — otherwise it's all too easy to get shiny-object syndrome and get completely derailed by focusing on tactics or tools that don't actually serve your plan.

Now, all your content — regardless of whether you're producing recurring content or content assets — needs to be focused around five pillars.

Pillar One: Simplicity

> *"Simplicity is the keynote of all true elegance."* — *Coco Chanel*

There's one thing that will make or break how a piece of content will perform, and that's the level of complexity. If you can't boil the topic down into something that's simple and easy to digest, you shouldn't use that topic. This is an extrapolation of Einstein's point that if you can't explain it simply, you don't understand it well enough.

Yes, some concepts are complex, and yes, some concepts require in-depth analysis and technical exploration. But even those topics can be addressed simply — and if you want people to come back to your content again, you'd better make it simple and easy to consume.

Now, some folks mistake 'simple' for 'stupid'. I'm not suggesting that your audience or customers are stupid. In fact, they're exactly the opposite. They're probably much smarter than you give them credit for. But smart people are usually busy people, looking for a smart solution, and this is where simplicity shines: they can immediately identify that your content holds the answer they're looking for. If you make it complex, they're likely to look elsewhere to find something easier. If you can sum it up for the reader instantly, they'll have an easy time saying yes to future content and offers from you. Of course, you need to use their language, understand their problems and motivations, and be willing to be generous and helpful.

But even if you do all that, it won't hook a single customer unless they can quickly grasp what you're talking about. Don't complicate your content with jargon or dense theoretical explanations to make yourself look smart. It just alienates people. You can dress it up a little, but you must be able to boil it down to the bare bones before you add anything more complex.

Pillar Two: Specificity

This is closely related to simplicity. Specificity in your content creates a self-selecting audience who will come back again and again for your specific solutions. If you're able to answer these questions for each piece of content you produce, you'll be in good shape (I'm including an example here in italics to demonstrate what I mean... and to be really specific):

- Who is reading this content? *The owner of a B2B service business.*
- What is the specific problem they are trying to solve by reading it? *Creating a consistent flow of qualified leads into their business.*
- What is the higher order consequence they want to achieve by reading this? *Building a predictable stream of revenue and stability into their business (and, by proxy, the rest of their lives).*
- What is the precise solution you can deliver that helps them achieve that outcome? *A step-by-step guide that shows them how to create content assets and systems that create traffic, capture leads and converts them into customers.*

Pillar Three: Serendipity

Jon Myers, a UX/UI designer I got to know in Vietnam, once told me to make room in my work for serendipity, and it's some of the best advice I've ever gotten. The more I pay attention to highly successful people, the more I hear this. Luck always plays a part, and it's no different when it comes to your content creation.

Chance, luck, the Universe conspiring, whatever you want to call it — sometimes things will fall into your lap and you have to be alert enough to grab them immediately. While I absolutely recommend having an editorial schedule, you should also have enough flexibility to change it quickly if something serendipitous happens.

Maybe you'll get featured somewhere and want to push the momentum as far as you can. Maybe you get to interview someone amazing and can publish it before anyone else gets the chance. Maybe a competitor screws up big time and you can capitalize on it.

Realize that opportunities like this come up all the time. Sometimes it turns up like an ugly duckling on your doorstep. Other times it's a golden egg tied up with a pretty bow. Sometimes it's the whole damn goose. Whatever it is, pay attention to what is really happening around you. Don't be so locked into your production schedule that you let serendipity pass you by.

The $10,000 Blog Post Case Study

In early 2015, I was working with a supplement brand who had spent a lot of resources differentiating themselves as the transparent provider of quality nutritional supplements.

That year Walmart, GNC, Target and Walgreens came under fire from the New York Attorney General's office. The supplements being sold in these giant chains had just been tested in independent research labs… and over half the products did not contain a single trace of any ingredient listed on the labels. Instead, they were stuffed with useless compounds, like ground up houseplants, rice powder and dried peas. And even worse? Some of these fillers were well-known allergens, like soybeans and peanuts. Beyond being outright misleading, this practice was dangerous to consumers and totally irresponsible.

As soon as the news broke, we leapt at the chance to create content around this big event. This is a critical part of creating content that converts: making your message timely and immediately useful. This is a prime example why it's key to have space in your content calendar for 'occasional' topics, and to keep space in your brain for serendipity.

I wrote a piece describing everything consumers needed to know about this situation, and published it within 48 hours of the news breaking. It covered all the information a consumer would want to know about the scandal and took a very strong stance. We condemned the practice and delved deep into how something like this could have happened, as well as why people need to boycott companies who mislead their customers.

This is the second key to creating powerful content: having an opinion. It's not enough to just state the facts – you have to let people know what you stand for, so they feel compelled to join your tribe or get the hell away from you. It also serves the purpose of educating your customers about something they're interested in, in turn making you a trusted authority in the space.

Finally, we promoted the article like our lives depended on it. In the good old days of the Internet, you could put up a blog post with a strong SEO title and people would just find it. But these days SEO saturation is at an all-time high, and people's attention is at a premium, so you need to be very proactive about promoting your content. We made sure there was a link to our website in the body copy, with a product placement ad in the sidebar, and we had pop-ups ready to go to collect email addresses from new visitors.

Then we boosted it on Facebook, our team posted it across all our social media networks, we shared it with influencers in our space, and we submitted it to sharing platforms like Reddit, Digg and StumbleUpon to increase the audience that would see it. Promoting a piece of timely, action-oriented content pays off: the post got over 700 shares on Facebook, our email list grew by 20%, and we made over $10,000 in sales in the next week directly from this post.

Even better? It's still making money. We added the post to an email onboarding sequence for new subscribers, as a way to differentiate ourselves from competitors. It's now one of the most highly trafficked pages on the client's blog, and continues to convert prospects into active buyers every week.

Pillar Four: Discipline

Serendipity has a way of showing up more often when you're putting in the work. Being disciplined about producing high-quality content creates high-quality opportunities. Finding the time for that work, though, is the biggest problem I hear about from business owners. They know they could make a real impact with their content. They know it's highly valuable information, and that they could probably crush their competition… if they could only be disciplined enough to get the words down.

It's not like they're slacking off, either. They're busy running their team, fulfilling orders, putting out fires… they just can't find the time to collect their thoughts, distill them into something simple and specific, and then actually sit down and write the damn stuff. It feels like it will take hours, every single week.

But that's the problem. Content works when you're consistent. You need to publish on a regular schedule to reap the full benefits, so you have to commit to the discipline of doing it, or find someone else to handle it for you.

If you do decide to produce your own content, you must pick ideas that inspire you. Picking *themes* that inspire you is even better, because a theme will allow you to come back to it again and again from different angles.

This is extremely important. It doesn't matter if you're the most disciplined person in the world. If the content is boring to you, you won't do it. It's true of anything. You don't do stuff you hate doing. Make it easy on yourself to be disciplined about it. Set a BIG vision for your business and the content it's built on, and then get after it on the regular. Only exciting, visionary ideas will energize you, attract the right customers to you, and keep you motivated to maintain your production schedule.

Pillar Five: Content Delegation

As the leader of your business, creating content might not be the highest and best use of your time, even if you do find themes that you're excited about. Having the discipline to do the work does *not* mean that you need to do everything yourself. Hiring someone who can help you with the actual deliverables is probably the highest leverage point you can create, especially if that person has a background in writing.

A client I now work with was spending close to 20 hours a week creating content. It didn't leave much time for getting new leads or closing more deals, but he is a stickler for excellent content…. he basically needed a clone.

Someone who got what was in his head and was able to create the same deliverables that he would.

To that end, he hired me. I've been through content marketing and conversion courses, publishing degrees and copywriting training. This has freed up all his time, and allowed him to focus on higher leverage activities that bring more customers into his business, while the content continues to be excellent quality and reliable for bringing in prospects for him to sell to.

Delegating content creation seems daunting at first. How could someone else possibly do as good a job as you would? How will they ever know what you know? But as I mentioned above, all you need is the right process for extracting the information from your head. Fortunately, that process is very simple and not quite as horrifying as 'extracting information from your head' makes it sound, and we'll get to that process later on.

Action Steps for Chapter Two:

1. Audit your current recurring content marketing:
   a. Do you have all six elements in place?
   b. If not, what would it take to have them built and implemented this quarter?
2. If you have (or are considering) a long-form content asset, does it have the four elements that would make it most successful?
   a. If not, what would it take to have them build and implemented this quarter?
3. Should you or your team be producing your content? Or would you be better served by outsourcing it to an expert who will produce high quality material while freeing up your time?

Chapter Three: Choose the Right Audience

"The aim of marketing is to know and understand the customer so well the product or service fits him and sells itself."
– Peter Drucker

There's a concept in copywriting that there are three elements to any successful campaign. First, you need the right audience. You need to be in front of people who know, like and trust you. You need to be positioned as someone they see as an authority, and there has to be goodwill present in the relationship that you can trade on. Secondly, you need the right offer. If you're going to go to the trouble of getting their attention, you have to have something to offer them that has real, tangible value. Don't dip into that goodwill unless it's going to be worth it, for you and for them. Finally, you need the right copy. You could have the world's *best* copywriter on your team, doing their very best work, but if the audience and offer aren't right, it will count for nothing. No copy will compensate for a disengaged list or mediocre offer. You have to have all three elements in place to have a successful campaign, but the most important of these is the audience.

In this section, we're going to delve into picking the right audience. To create a successful, evergreen content marketing strategy, you need a deep understanding of the people you are selling to (and evergreen content should be where you focus most of your efforts — content that holds its value over time, that doesn't date badly, and that continues to be useful to your audience regardless of when they read it. This is particularly important if you're creating long-form content that takes a lot of resources to build).

Now, customers vary massively between different kinds of B2B businesses. For large industrial companies, for example, the customer is the wholesaler, retailer or purchasing department from another business — not an end user. The offer and copy, then, need to be focused on the people making the buying decisions. It's their responsibility to then market it accurately to the consumer. If you own a B2B *service* business, though, you often deal directly with the customer, and will often come into contact with your customer's customers. In that scenario, you need to understand how your marketing affects your customers directly, and how it trickles down to *their* customers.

Most people in B2B services have a rough idea of who their ideal customers are, but they don't have a clearly defined persona that they can build a marketing strategy around. For example, you might say *"Well, my customers are ecommerce owners who have over $2 million in annual revenue."* That's a start, sure, but it's woefully incomplete. There are thousands of ecommerce businesses which would fit that criteria, but for one reason or another, many of them would be a terrible fit for your services. Maybe their team is too big or too small. Maybe the owners are in conflict. Maybe they have investors complicating their processes. Maybe they sell products that don't jive with your ethics or brand. Maybe they don't have the budget to work with you. Maybe they already have the solution you're offering. Without a clearly defined outline of your ideal customers and their needs, you're stuck before you've even started. That's why developing a customer avatar is such an important exercise.

Why You Need a Customer Avatar

The concept of a customer avatar has been in marketing forever, but it's gained a lot of momentum in the last few years as the online space has become more sophisticated and marketers talk about it more. The purpose behind developing a customer avatar is to develop a deep understanding of the motivations, fears, desires, and problems that influence customer buying decisions. In creating a profile that indicates the customer's priorities, goals and challenges, you can tailor your positioning and offers to serve them best.

To be clear: you are always going to have multiple types of customers. People are too complex to be categorized down into a single tidy box that predicts all their behaviors. You will probably have several types of people who will want your services. Your priority here, though, is to identify your *primary* customer — the person for whom your service is a no-brainer and who will get great returns on their investment with you. The Harvard Business Review[2] recommends a three-fold approach to identifying if a market segment is right for your business: perspective, capabilities and profit potential.

Assessing perspective is about making sure the customer's attitudes fit with yours. You want to make sure that they have similar priorities, sensibilities and direction to you. For example, Apple is renowned for its total obsession with design and usability. Their customers are also highly attentive to design and experience, so Apple's product and marketing teams know exactly who they need to get their products in front of. Amazon is relentless in its focus on providing amazing shopping experiences, and so they attract customers who prioritize great service and convenience. The perspectives between the business and the customer are aligned.

Assessing for capabilities is about the 'embedded resources' of your company. These are the assets and resources that position your business to serve one type of customer better than another. For example, your business might have

---

[2] https://hbr.org/2014/03/choosing-the-right-customer

really strong or innovative technology, highly visible brand equity and marketing, or industry-specific capabilities that other companies have trouble competing with. Any one of those elements make your business much more valuable to a particular type of customer over others. Determining whether your capabilities fit with the perspective and profit potential is key to choosing the right audience.

Last but certainly not least is the profit potential of your chosen market. Do they have budgets that will accommodate your prices? Is your service likely to bring them a sufficiently significant return that it's a no-brainer for them to work with you? Is there enough growth potential in *their* businesses for you to raise your prices and maintain them as paying customers? Are there other things they need that you can add to your services in order to increase your profit margins?

Now that you have a conceptual framework of the type of audience you're looking for, let's look at how you build a specific customer avatar.

B2B Customer Avatar Development

Background:
- What is this person's experience in this industry?
- What are they responsible for?
- What is the profile of their company (revenue, headcount, trajectory)

Demographic:
- Age, gender
- Income
- Family status
- Location

Identifiers:

- Position in the company
- Preferred communication channel

Goals:

- What motivates them at work? (i.e. delivering a profit, being seen as innovative, valuable to the company etc)
- What's the main responsibility in their role?
- What's their professional biggest opportunity? Biggest risk?
- What's their major fear or anxiety in their role?
- What's their ambition beyond their current position?

Challenges:

- What is hard or impossible for them to do themselves or in-house?
- Where do they get resistance or push-back at work?
- What pressures or problems are they facing from the rest of their team?
- What pressures or problems are they facing from their industry and competitors?

Influences:

- Who do they pay attention to? Who's the *"If so-and-so says it, I'll do it"* person?
- Where do they get their information from? What are their go-to websites, podcasts, and books?

How you help them:

- What part of their job do you make easier?
- What problems do you handle for them?

- How do you make them look good?

Their key objections:

- Logistics?
- Budget?
- Lack of authority?
- Don't think it will work?

Action Steps For Chapter Three

1. Get a pen and paper and think of a market segment you've done work with. Assess them for perspective, capability fit and profit potential. Is there a sufficiently good fit for you to commit to focus on working just with that segment? If not, repeat the exercise until you find a segment that fits the criteria.

2. Go through the customer avatar development list. Think of the customers you've had the best experiences with in the past, and model the avatar for your primary customer on them. Remember that your primary customer is the one you actively build your marketing and business development around.

3. Repeat the avatar exercise for secondary and tertiary customers. These are the customers who will want your service but are not the people you actively pursue in your marketing.

Chapter Four: Make the Right Offers

Once you're in front of the right people, the next step is to ensure that you're making the right offers. Your offers — the products or services that your company offers to its market — should be tailored to your primary customer. This is critical. You can't be all things to all people. Yes, your secondary and tertiary customers will most likely want your offer regardless, but you are positioning it for your primary buyers. The primary buyers are the people that matter most, and now that you've done all the work to identify them, it's time to give them what they want.

Now, let me spell out why we're talking about audience and offers in a book about content marketing. Well, without those two things nailed down, you've really got nothing to market and no one to market to. These are two of the most critical element of successful marketing, so it's important to realize that marketing begins long before you ever publish a blog post or run an ad. I can't stress this enough. It's critically important that you are clear about your audience and your offer.

To identify the types of offers that are most likely to be a success with your market, you must go back to your primary customers. Understanding their needs, problems and motivations will help you settle quickly on the offers that will serve them. Is their business struggling to carve out market share? A book on powerful positioning and branding will be a hit. Are they losing money hand over fist because their staff churn is huge? A course on training employees for long-term loyalty will be a no-brainer. Maybe they're losing revenue to aggressive competitors — a business development workshop will be just what they need.

Yes, there's a degree of trial and error in developing the best offer for your audience, and it can take some time for the perfect option to materialize. There might be multiple offers that will serve them well, but you'll usually see varying degrees of impact. For example, a client of mine offered one-to-one business development coaching. He would assess the entire business, from operations to marketing to executive hiring. This was a huge boon for his clients… but after a while he realised that the most powerful service he could offer was leadership training for businesses that were at a tipping point in their growth. This allowed to him to work with only the most successful of his primary customers, and to charge a whole lot more for what amounted to less work. That's the kind of offer where everyone wins, and that's exactly what you want to be working towards.

In order to settle on an offer like this for your business, you must have an iron grasp on what matters most to your primary customers. In some markets, they will value economical pricing. Others will want speed of implementation. Others will want pure performance, and others will care most about appearance, or efficiency, or optimization. You have to know them in order to pinpoint what the most valuable thing you can offer them will be.

How to Develop The Right Offer For Your Audience

> *"There are no facts inside your building, so get outside"*
> — *Steve Blank, author of The Startup Owner's Manual.*

Product development — whether it's a physical product, a consulting service or a digital course — requires patience and finesse. Many businesses (particularly young businesses that operate online) do not approach their offers with the level of care that's required to build something truly powerful. While there's definitely value in getting to market quickly, and in shipping a product when it's good enough, oftentimes those attitudes are taken to extremes that damage the brand and leave customers cold. Getting this right is even more important when your audience is made up of 'digital natives' who think nothing of jumping on Twitter to slam you when their expectations are not met.

In the early days of Facebook, "Move fast and break things" was the go-to motto. And it's true that Seth Godin implores businesses to "always be shipping." But like so many things on the internet, both of those catchy sound bites can be taken *way* out of context… and many businesses have gone under because they took them too literally.

*(Personally, I think Godin must feel like someone is walking on his grave every time a business throws a product out the door screaming "IT'S SHIPPED", given that his actual intent was to get the **best** product into the market on a predetermined date, rather than getting **anything** out as soon as possible. See The Ship It Journal[3] for more clarity on this.)*

Short of knowing and understanding your audience, developing the right products is the most important thing you can possibly do for your business. Your offerings are the very foundations your company is built on, and just throwing something together for the sake of having something to sell is not the right way to build something that could last your whole lifetime and beyond.

Market validation, then, is a critical part of developing the right offers for your audience. How will you know what your market wants, if you never talk to

---

[3] https://sethgodin.typepad.com/files/theshipitjournal.pdf

them? How do you know if people will buy what you're selling if you've never asked them if they're interested, or if this product would solve a real problem they are actually experiencing? Yes, it's scary to talk to real people, and yes, it's super annoying to wait for feedback when you have an idea that you think is really great... but it will save you so much time, money and heartache to get this right from the outset.

Here are the key steps you need to take *before* you start developing a product or offering.

Step One: Get the Facts

You know the old saying that you've got two ears and one mouth, so that we can listen twice as much as we speak? Nowhere is that more true than in product development. You can talk and talk about what you *think* your customers want and need, but until you shut it and let them *tell* you specifically, you're running blind. You might have a pretty good idea about their problems and the solutions they want, but listening to your customers will bring nuance and clarity to your offering that will usually be the difference between mediocre uptake and run-away success. Or, you might find that you were way off, and that you'd do much better offering something else entirely.

You can do this a number of ways. Start by surveying them. Ask them questions that will help you quickly see if your assumptions are correct, if they're using your product or service as you think they are, and what the offer is doing for them. These questions will help you to find out whether your beliefs about your customers are accurate, and whether or not they want what you're currently offering them:

- Why did you choose to use [product/service]?

- How are you using [product/service]?
- What is the key problem it solves for you?
- What are some secondary problems it solves?
- How has it made life easier for you?
- What's the best thing about it? What would you change?
- Did you consider other solutions before choosing ours? What made you choose us?
- What were your doubts or concerns before choosing us? What questions did you have that weren't addressed?
- What else do you think we should know or be doing?
- If you were telling a friend about this, what would you say to them?

If you don't have a customer base yet, find people who fit your primary customer avatar and reframe these questions around the hypothetical product or service you're planning to offer (*"Would you use this product? What would you use it for? What would it do for you? What would it feature to serve you best? How much would you pay for it?"*).

Step 2: Simplify

Simplicity, always. If you can't explain your offer in two or three sentences, it's too complicated and is not sufficiently clear to win the attention (and dollars) of your primary customers. You should speak enough of their lexicon, and understand them well enough, that you can immediately articulate the solution you are presenting to their problem. While it's tempting to believe that more complex solutions seem more impressive to customers, it's rarely the case. The more complicated something seems, the less likely the customer is to pay attention. Humans always look for the path of least resistance — if something is hard, or requires a lot of attention from us to work, we don't want to deal with it. We like easy, so give your customers easy.

Step 3: Review

Review regularly. Markets change, and you have to keep up in order to stay afloat. One of the most damaging things in business is the 'set and forget' mentality. Sure, it works for basic tasks that can be replicated, but not when it comes to your offers or customers. So many businesses resist this fact: your work is not done once you settle on a product and a group of people to sell to.

There are any number of things that can disrupt what your market segment wants and needs. For example, if a new player enters the market and their offer crushes yours, you a) want to see it coming and be prepared, and b) be ready to offer something new or improved. A new piece of technology might make part of your service redundant. You might be so great at what you do that you work yourself out of a job, in which case you need to develop another product that allows you to retain your clients and maximize their lifetime value.

Sometimes it won't be that drastic. You might be able to add a feature that significantly improves your customer retention. You might be able to remove something that significantly improves your profit margin. Small changes can be as powerful as big ones. In order to identify those potential changes, though, you need to regularly take stock of your offer and your market. It can be tough to be objective about your business, and to trust the numbers or what you're hearing from customers who aren't necessarily 'experts', but it's key to the health of your business.

Action Steps for Chapter Four

1. Write down all your assumptions about how the offer will suit your audience: what problem they are trying to solve, the best way you can

help them do that, and how you think that should be packaged up (including the positioning, pricing and production).

2. Put together a survey based on the questions in earlier in this chapter. List all the questions in an online form and send it to customers who have agreed to respond (Typeform or Google Forms are very easy to get set up with, and they look professional). You can invite your best customers to participate, or you can send it to your whole social media following and/or email list. You can also contact people who you think would be your ideal customers and ask them to get involved. Regardless of where you get your participants, try to offer them some sort of incentive for responding so that they are more willing to get involved. Bonus content tends to work well — worksheets that help them work out something practical for their business, access to educational recordings or videos, or resources that you usually only share with clients.

3. Collect all the answers and set them aside for a few days. Take some time out so you can sit quietly and go through all the responses. Grab a coffee at a nice sunny cafe and get ready: you might be surprised at what you find. You may need to be ready to work some changes into your business. You may not be surprised at all, in which case you're obviously doing something very right, or have made adjustments already that have put you on the right path... or you might get sledgehammered, and be forced to recognize that there's a lot of change that needs to happen in your business if it's going to work. Whatever it is, take the time to delve deep into the responses and map out what they mean for your offers.

4. Brainstorm some ideas for offers that will give your customers what they want and need, *and* that will maximize your customer lifetime value. Send these ideas to all the participants and ask them which of those options they would actually want to use, and how much they would pay for it. Not only does this give you real clarity about what the market wants, but it gives you an opportunity to *sell* that offer to those people immediately. You can sell it at 'beta testing' prices and create the product as you go along (if it's a course or digital program) or use the crowdfunding model to take those early payments and use them to develop the product. Only create your product when you know what the market wants.

Chapter Five: Get Your Messaging Right

When it comes to content strategy, most people start with copywriting. They put together ads and sales letters, blog posts and emails…. But they have no idea who they're talking to. Copywriting is a critical skill in your content marketing, and we'll be talking about it in depth later on this book, but it is one of the final elements for you to nail down. You must settle on your primary customer profile first, then develop the right offers, and then get your overall messaging strategy pinned down before you should touch any copywriting. Creating powerful, compelling messaging — whether it's sales copy, blog content or social media updates — depends entirely on knowing who you're talking to, what their problem is, and how you're going to solve it.

Messaging is the overarching voice, intent and positioning of *all* the content that comes out of your business. Businesses regularly produce a huge amount of content without even realizing it. Of course, some content is obvious….

- Blog posts
- Social media updates
- Podcasts
- YouTube videos
- Email funnels

But other types of content are less obvious, because they're not necessarily part of a 'content marketing strategy', and so there can be a lot of variation in the messaging that is coming out of one company. These less obvious forms of content include…

- Interviews
- Press releases
- Customer communications
- Website content (including home page content, About pages, Product/Services pages)
- Opt-in or acquisition assets…

Any piece of content that comes out of your business or is associated with your brand should have consistent messaging.

(Your messaging needs to be balanced across all the different kinds of content coming out of your business. This includes the visual messaging, such as including your logo, branding each page with the same colour schemes and layouts, and so on. It's very important that there is continuity every time the customer interacts with your brand — it creates a sense of familiarity and trust. Unless you're doing it intentionally to get a particular reaction, you never want to jar someone with an incongruent or unexpected piece of content.)

Your audience is the most important factor in deciding on the messaging for your brand: who are you speaking to? Is your audience the middle-aged corporate suite of publicly listed companies? Or is your audience made up of the late-twenties founders of small, scrappy start-ups who have just closed their first rounds of funding? I can't overstate this enough — you must know who your audience is in order to be able to communicate with them in a way that will eventually get a conversion from them.

Psychology, Self-Perception and Language

Once you have a clear profile of who your primary customer is, you need to identify what affects their psychology, how they perceive themselves, and what kind of language they use. Are the individuals you deal with directly motivated by wanting to look good in front of their colleagues and getting lots of recognition, or are they driven to achieve by a crippling fear of failure? Try to find the nuances that let you get inside the mind of your customers.

It's not always easy to get to these core drives, but going through the customer avatar exercise in Chapter Three will give you a good starting point. Short of setting up a therapist's couch in your office and inviting your prospects to a session, you might have to do a little bit of extrapolation from conversations you've had with ideal clients before. What have clients told you previously that they're worried about? What have they let slip that gave you an insight into the world behind the professional facade? What are their priorities? What do they think they need to learn or acquire to get to their ideal outcome? You can expand on past customer experiences to predict future client experiences.

In B2B messaging, there are a few 'models' that you might come across in customer psychology. The people in the businesses you're dealing with might have…

- A deep-seated need to…
    - Prove themselves to authority figures or leaders
    - Get attention and be in the spotlight
    - Be perceived as a champion or high-value asset to the business
    - Beat others so as not to be seen as being lower down the foodchain
    - Maintain the status quo to preserve their position

- A paralyzing fear of…
    - Being exposed as a fraud (even if they're not one)
    - Failure (on any scale)
    - Public humiliation (in the eyes of the general public)
    - Private humiliation (in the eyes of people who know them)

- An unquenchable appetite for…
    - Money
    - Power
    - Freedom (not having to answer to anyone)
    - Fame and reputation

There are also external pressures being brought to bear on your customers all the time:

- Differentiating themselves and remaining competitive in their market
- Dealing with new competitors in their market
- Implementing adjustments in market regulation
- Handling increases, downturns or adjustments in consumer behaviors
- Anticipating changes, opportunities or threats in their market

◆ ◆ ◆

Once you understand what makes your primary customer tick, it's much easier to create a messaging strategy that speaks directly to them. The language used in that messaging will usually be demographic dependent: are they young, middle-aged, elderly? Are they college-educated, or did they apprentice in a trade? Are they wordy philosophical types, or are they straight-shooters? If you're addressing the 50-year-old members of the corporate suite of an established company, you're going to encounter a very different lexicon to what you find talking to the Millennial founders of a start-up — the language you use to position your brand should depend entirely on who is going to be absorbing it.

Not only does the language vary between demographics, but the perspectives on their industry will be different, the priorities within the business will be different, and the values they're focused on will be different — you need to understand how they perceive the world in order to develop messaging that lands with them.

The founders of a young start-up will also have very different priorities to the board or C-suite of a publicly listed company. The start-up will be focused on speed to market, product validation, and (hopefully) defensibility, whereas the C-level guys are going to more focused on efficiency, covering liabilities, maintaining market share (though if they're the incumbent in an industry that's about to be disrupted, their priorities will be different again).

Getting to understand the market your customers are playing in is also key to getting your messaging right: it's not just about the individuals, it's also about understanding their industry. Understand the internal pressures they're exerting on themselves, but also the external pressures they're facing on a regular basis.

Messaging relies in part on your positioning and perception in your marketplace. If you are the 'authority leader' in your industry, with years and years of experience, then you can use a weighty, authority-driven kind of messaging. If you're a newcomer to the scene, disrupting the way things are done, then you can use a more cheeky or lighthearted messaging. Getting to understand your place in the market you're operating in will help to define your messaging. That's not to say that industry is the only consideration — who you are as people should also come through. Customers want to know who they're dealing with, so let them know! Tell your story, highlight your team, and share your successes. Give your customers a sense of who you are, how they can relate to you and why you'll be more fun (or effective, or fast) to work with than anyone else.

Ultimately, if you understand your audience and your offer, the messaging will fall into place naturally, even if you're not a great writer (though we'll go into the specifics of how to write great content and copy towards the end of this book). The most important thing is being able to communicate what is important to your customers in a way that makes them comfortable with you. Once you've grasped that, you'll be able to position all your marketing accurately, which is half the job done.

Communication is at the very core of every healthy relationship — and make no mistake, your business is about relationships. While I think you're going to get a lot out of this book, I'd be happy if that is the only thing you really take to heart... so I'll say it again:

Business is about people and your relationship with them. Clear communication is the most important skill you can develop to make the relationship successful.

Not only does great communication make you a trustworthy source, but it makes you a real authority. It creates a loyalty in your audience that most companies can only dream of. Great communication makes it impossible to ignore you and will bring in deeply committed customers over the long term who are willing to spend a lot of money with you.

Action Steps for Chapter Five

1. Audit your most recent content (say, from the last two weeks), including all emails, blog content, social media content, press releases, and anything else you regularly publish, and create a list of consistencies and inconsistencies that emerge from comparing it all.

2. What are the themes that have emerged from this comparison? Do you think customers are getting the right message from all the content coming out of your business?

3. What kind of language does your primary customer use? What's their style of communication, and what's their vocabulary? Is it technical or emotive? Formal or relaxed?

4. Compare the language from your content audit with the language profile of your primary customer. Do they match up? If not, what needs to change in your messaging to mirror the language your customers use, to create the rapport you need in your communications? If it does match up, is there anything you can improve on further?

Chapter Six: Creating Your Recurring Content

Once you've nailed down your audience, offer and messaging, you can start work on your actual content. Recurring content (such as blogging, podcasting, YouTube videos) is what comes to mind for most people when they think about content marketing. Unfortunately, many people confuse 'publishing' with 'marketing' and they end up getting completely stuck as result. You see, publishing lots of content does not a marketer make: if you don't have a plan behind the content you're putting out (a plan that includes collecting contact details, sending onboarding or follow-up content, and sending targeted sales offers), you will never make money or gain the loyal following that content is supposed to create for you.

Now, the reason so many people get stuck here is that you *can* produce content without making sales offers. With other marketing strategies like PPC (pay-per-click advertising) or SEO (search engine optimization), where you make a financial investment, you can see very tangibly that you're just throwing your money away if you don't make specific sales offers. Content marketing can be a refuge for business owners who want to feel good about 'doing some marketing' but who are scared of sales and are resisting overcoming those fears.

Let me lay this out here: If you use content creation to feel productive while you avoid selling, you will go broke.

You have to make sales offers for people to convert, no matter what kind of marketing you are doing, and content is no different. You cannot avoid this and expect *any* marketing to work for you. Sales bring in the money, not marketing. Marketing just gets people to pay attention, so that you can offer them the sale.

So: to create recurring content that will capture the attention of your market, and then leverage that attention into real sales conversions, you need to create a *conversion opportunity*. In this chapter that we're going to go deep into how you do that.

Here are the six elements again of a recurring content marketing strategy that will create conversions:

- High quality front-end content (either blogs, podcasts, videos or social media updates
- A front-end opt-in offer (like an email course, industry report, cheat sheet)
- An email onboarding sequence
- An initial sales offer
- A follow-up sequence
- More sales offers

You want to create a situation where people a) have an opportunity to convert on something early in their relationship with you, b) can convert again at a higher price point later on, and c) refer people to you that will *also* convert. This cyclical model can create a strong sales cycle in your business over time.

Choose Your Front-End Content Themes

Content tends to perform best when it is produced on a regular schedule. For most businesses, one piece of quality content per week is enough (although if your main platform is social media, it needs to be much more frequent, usually a few posts per day). Here's a common scenario I hear about when talking to business owners:

"I try to publish every week on Tuesdays. I sit down on Monday or Tuesday morning to come up with something, and I end up getting distracted and frustrated because I don't know what to write about. It just falls down my to-do list and then I get to the end of the week and I still haven't done anything."

That is a horrible, discouraging feeling. Not only have you wasted your time, missed a marketing opportunity and raised your blood pressure, you've also failed to deliver something your audience is expecting from you, which damages your credibility. This cycle is hard to break, and it becomes a self-fulfilling prophecy: you don't know what to produce, so you get frustrated. You feel frustrated, so you don't want to do it anymore. You don't want to do it, so you feel resistant and resentful every time you sit down to do it.

If that's where you're at, STOP. Just stop. You won't do something you hate, no matter how good it would be for your business.

Here's what to do instead. Read through all your customer service tickets and your conversations with prospects. Work out what the most common questions are, and what you're explaining over and over again. Think about what you want to be known for, what your unique sales proposition is, and what your customers want from you. Boil all that down into three or four broad themes that you can come back to over and over again from different perspectives. For example, if you have a business operations consultancy, your key themes might be…

- How to increase throughput in production facilities
- How to manage staff
- How to scale operations without breaking them
- How to deal with external partners

Each of those themes has many, many subtopics you can explore in your weekly content, whether it's on your blog, YouTube channel, podcast or social media. At the beginning of each quarter, sit down and map out three to four subtopics for which you can create content under the umbrella of each of those main themes. Write out a couple of potential headlines for each, as well as mapping out four or five key points to touch on within each post. Put all this in a spreadsheet, along with the projected publication date (and you can find a basic template for this under the Quarterly Content Plan at laurahanly.com/ctc-resources).

That way, when you sit down to produce the content each week, you've already got a plan. Having a plan is the simplest way to get it done — you don't waste any time looking around for a topic, discarding talking points or staring at a blank screen. The hardest part is already done, and you can sit down, look at the topic for the week, and start working through each of the bullet points immediately. (That said, I do recommend starting this a few days before you're due to publish, so that the pressure of a hard deadline is not bearing down on you.)

Alongside these regular themes, you can also make a list of 'occasional' topics. These are things you want to touch on every now and then – either to remind your market about something you do, to make a sales offer, or to add something fresh to the conversations and events happening in your industry.

I recommend covering each of your main themes once per month, and one of the 'occasional' topics each four to six weeks. This formula establishes you as the go-to authority for your pillar competencies, while keeping your readers on their toes with your occasional posts.

To get into the technical details of the planner, you can either make a copy of the spreadsheet on the Resources page, or build your own spreadsheet with the start-date of each week, as well as the day of the week you plan to publish. In the next cell, add in the specific topic that's going to be covered for that week, and any keywords or sub-topics you want to hit. You can write the actual title of the post if you prefer, just to keep everything clear in your head (and in any communications you might have about each post with your team).

Finally, add in who is going to be writing the post (if it's not you), and whether the post is scheduled for distribution. This includes email distribution to your mailing list, social media scheduling, sharing with the influencers in your market, adding to forums, sending to specific contacts etc. If you publish something, you need to make sure you spend some time to actually get it in front of the people you want to have consuming it.

As Jonah Peretti says, content is king but distribution is queen, and she wears the pants (and he would know, having led BuzzFeed for nearly a decade now and saturated just about every newsfeed ever). Your content doesn't have to be long, it doesn't have to have glossy post-production or be overly complicated. It *does* need to be interesting and useful, and it does have to be engaging and visible. The content you produce should give away the farm.

Don't hold anything back from your audience. Let them see exactly how you do business, what your processes and perspectives are, and show them that you're a real authority by sharing everything you know.

Build An Opt-In Offer

If you spend much time online, particularly in internet marketing circles, you can't avoid hearing about the 'powers' of content marketing. To hear some people talk about it, you would think they'd found the fountain of youth and a vault full of money right beside it… but content on its own is just not enough. Yes, it's powerful because it can cut through the noise online and shows your visitors that you can be trusted. But if you're going to build a relationship with those visitors, you've got to have a way to continue communicating with them regularly. You can't assume they'll remember to check your blog every week or that they'll buy from you unprompted.

Thanks to our intensely information-rich modern lifestyle, it's harder than ever to judge what's right and useful. People are desperate for transparency and trust in their relationships, and that goes double for the businesses they deal with. Content, paired with ongoing communication, gives you the best opportunity you will ever have to give that to people. When you can give people the transparency and genuine help they are looking for, they'll be yours for life… if you implement the system I'm about to tell you about.

Most content is distributed on platforms you do not own — Facebook, Twitter, content networks, search engines and so on. Those platforms own the traffic, and if they change how they do business, you can lose your audience. That's why it's critical to start building a contact list that you own and can market to directly. This is where opt-in offers come into play. Whenever a new person visits your site, they should have the opportunity to join your mailing list or private community in exchange for some incentive. You need to get their email address or have them set up an account so that you can build up a profile for them over time, communicate with them directly, and make carefully targeted sales offers to them when the time is right.

Your opt-in offers do not need to be cripplingly complex. This is a critical aspect of a content marketing strategy, so let me be clear: Done is better than perfect. Assets like this can always be more detailed, or have a longer word-count, or be more testimonial-heavy, but once you have a good piece of information that's useful, polished and appealing, publish it. Every day you do not have an active opt-in is a day you are losing leads, and wasting the resources you've put into creating your content so far. Ideally, you would give the subscriber a piece of premium content, but at the very least, a pop-up box that asks for their email address will do (use SumoMe.com to get that set up).

Here are some asset types for compelling opt-in offers:

- Industry report or white paper
- Case study
- Video series
- Webinar
- Demo
- Discount code
- Quiz or survey
- Cheat sheet
- How-to guide
- Industry or client profiles

Pick the type of asset most appropriate to your industry, and based on what your customers will value. Make sure that it's better information than they would usually find in your public content, and make it feel high-quality wherever possible, so that they're impressed and want to see what comes next. The offer should also have a clear benefit for the subscriber: take care to communicate the value they are going to get as a result of giving you their information, and that you set their expectations accurately before they opt in. Make sure the asset is delivered to them immediately, via a thank-you page and/or a confirmation email.

Build an Onboarding Sequence

Getting someone's email address or having them create an account is a big win. This is a micro-commitment from them (which is the first step towards having them buy from you), as well as getting their permission to market to them. This is huge, and you want to capitalize on this opportunity. An email onboarding sequence creates a window for you to do that. Onboarding, also referred to as 'organizational socialization', is done through an automated sequence of emails by which subscribers are educated about your brand, engaged with your community, and indoctrinated with your values.

Most onboarding sequences are between four and eight emails long, depending on your industry and offerings. If you are in a highly competitive industry, and have a complex solution, then you probably need a more in-depth sequence than a business that has little competition or a simple offer.

Here's a templated structure you can use for a general onboarding sequence. If someone has opted in to receive something, these are some general topics for the emails you might send them:

- Email one: Welcome! We're glad you've joined us. Here is the thing you opted in for, and here are few more resources to get you started, with a bit of info about us.
- Email two: Common problems in the industry, and how some of our customers (who are just like you) have overcome them.
- Email three: Bonus tips to deal with difficult industry things
- Email four: What we do and why it's going to be great for you
- Email five: Answer FAQs in depth. PS — want to get on a call / book a demo / join a webinar?
- Email six: Customer success stories and testimonials
- Email seven: Book in your freecall / demo / webinar today: benefit, benefit, benefit, testimonial
- Email eight: We noticed you haven't booked your free thing yet — was it something we said?

(We'll go into further depth on how to build your onboarding sequences later on in this book.)

The goal of this sequence is to establish yourself as an authority on the topic they opted in to hear about, and to get them to take the next step with you. Whether it's booking a call, taking a demo, joining a webinar or even just replying to an email, make sure you're positioning the subscriber to engage. This is mission-critical. Never assume that a prospect will read all your information and then decide on their own to get in touch or make a purchase. They won't. People need to be led, so make sure you have something specific you are leading them towards. You never want someone to be unclear about what their next step should be. This is true at any point as the customer is moving through your ecosystem, but *particularly* at this stage when they've been exposed to your ideas and expertise, and it's time for them to make a purchasing decision.

Common 'next steps' in a B2B business would be one of the following, depending on the nature of your market, your offering and the messaging that works best:

- Invite them to a free webinar. A lot of marketers do this extremely well — people like Frank Kern, Noah Kagan and Ryan Levesque leverage webinars to engage people to great success all the time. This format works so well because it allows the marketer to give a lot of value up front, without requiring a large time investment from the prospect. Webinars are also a direct platform to sell from, as they basically create a captive audience: the prospect joins the webinar, learns lots of good stuff, and then (with the principle of reciprocity working quietly in the back of their mind) will sit through a sales pitch even if they don't have to. At this point, the prospect is primed: they think of you as an approachable authority who is speaking directly to their problems, and so you can offer them your solution while they are right there in a receptive frame of mind.

- Offer them a free demo. This works in a similar way to the webinar model, but works particularly well for SaaS (software as a service) businesses, and companies that offer some kind of technical solution. We built a free demo offer into the onboarding email sequence for Wicked Reports, and they saw a significant uptick in both booked demos and sales. Having been educated up to a point about the power of the product, their prospects become very curious to see the tool in action in a few different scenarios, and are therefore willing to book in an hour to get to know Wicked Reports better. Most people learn well in a visual format, so seeing the tool in use is a powerful way to move them towards a conversion. You know the old saying *"possession is nine-tenths of the law"*? Well, an interactive demo is about as close as you can get to having the prospect 'possess' the product. If you can demonstrate your offer in action, they're going to be much more likely to take the next step you want.

- Invite them to a free call. This works particularly well for consultants and service businesses, because often the offer is a little less tangible than what's being sold in other B2B businesses. Make it clear that it's an obligation-free call, and that they can spend as much time as they want asking questions, picking apart your offer and really getting a feel for whether you're the right fit for them. It's an opportunity for them to air any skepticism, get clarity about what they need, and get to know you. A very powerful part of the onboarding process is that they get sufficiently educated about your product or process that they feel comfortable getting on the phone with you, because they will know what they're talking about. You never want someone to come into a conversation like this blind, because the power balance is too much in your favor. In that situation, the prospect can feel like you hold all the cards and they don't have enough information to assess whether you're being straight with them. This makes people feel defensive, and wary of you trying to 'put it over them'. You want to make sure they have a locus of control in the interaction so that they're comfortable and more open to the conversation. Before getting on the phone with anyone, make sure they have as much information as they need, and let them know that you encourage a critical approach in your customers, that you only want to work with people who take their business seriously, and that you're not going to put a hard sell on them.

All the content that you produce up to this point should be driving the prospect towards having some kind of real-time interaction with you. Business is about people, and people won't do anything if trust and rapport is missing from an interaction. They need to relate to you as a person they can trust; who will be a positive influence in their business, and will ultimately help them fill whatever deep-seated need is driving them.

(And make no mistake — it's rarely a cut and dry desire to make more money that drives people. Some want status, others want recognition, others still want positive feedback... there's a whole neurochemical chain reaction going on when someone makes a buying decision, and while that's beyond the scope of this book, we'll be getting into a little bit of the behavioral psychology that should factor into your marketing later on.)

Carlos Ruiz Zafón, one of the most popular Spanish novelists of the modern age, says that we only accept as true what can be narrated. Knowing, then, that people will only buy what you're selling when it's wrapped up in a story or narrative that resonates with them, you need to find a way to position your content in a way that does that. Your offer should be presented as a story they can see themselves taking an active part in, and you yourself should be presented as a narrator they trust and find relatable.

Understanding that, you should always be driving them to some sort of interactive action. This is a critical aspect of high-converting content: there's always a clear call to action that moves them further through your funnel. The prospect is never left alone without a clear next step, they'll never wonder if you have some hidden ulterior motive — they know and trust you, because you told them the story they needed to hear. This is why knowing deeply who your audience is, what offer they need to receive, and how to position your messaging, is the cornerstone of creating high-converting content.

Next, we're going to dive into the most critical steps of all — making sales offers and following up with your prospects.

Make Sales Offers

The secret to creating content that converts is to create a conversion moment. Yes, despite all the progress that marketing has made, you still have to make sales offers if you want to convert your prospects. There's no marketing system in the world that can extract a sale without first making a sales offer.

All businesses live and die by the number of sales they make. It doesn't matter how good your systems are, or if you have a great team, or you've got unrivalled SOPs… it doesn't even matter if you have hyper-focused marketing and a replicable lead acquisition funnel. If you don't make sales offers, it's all for nothing.

Of the dozens of B2B businesses I've worked with over the years, just one thing separates the success stories from the failures, and it's that the leaders of the company committed to sales. They committed to making the offer every time — they committed to ignoring their fear of rejection, their anxiety about pissing people off, and the voice in their head that said they couldn't do it. They committed, consistently made their offers, and came out on top because of it.

Sales offers come in all shapes and sizes, depending on the business. You might invite someone to book a paid consult with you, or you might offer them an ongoing service for which they pay you every month. You might offer them the purchase of a single unit, or the purchase of thousands of units. You might offer them paid access to a piece of software that will automate part of their business. Whatever it is, you need to explicitly offer to give them your product or service in return for a specific amount of money.

If you are afraid of making sales offers off the back of your content, or you 'sell from your heels' (making a half-hearted attempt at a sale that doesn't really showcase the benefits, or ask the prospect for an answer), your content will never convert a single customer. You will be wasting all your resources and in time, your business will fail.

I understand how uncomfortable this part of the process can be. Most people who run their own businesses have a host of private fears and doubts that stop them from selling. Fears of…

- Being 'uncovered' as a fraud
- Being rejected
- Being found lacking in either their qualifications or what they're offering
- Being perceived as pushy, rude, or mercenary
- Being unable to deliver what they are offering

Usually, these fears are completely unfounded, and they're all rooted in the fundamental human need to be accepted by your tribe. It's horrible to think that someone you pitch would be offended by your offer, and then go and rip on you all over the internet... but with a content ecosystem that gradually entices people to your offer, sharing information that benefits them and shows that you have their best interests in mind, you're not going to get that kind of treatment.

The great thing about the content ecosystem is that most of the people you will speak to will be pre-qualified as a potential buyer, so they're likely to respond positively to an offer. The best approach in this case is usually not a hard sell, but a simple mention of 'here's what I've got, here's what it will do for you, and here's how to get it.'

In fact, I've never had a client have a bad reaction from their customers when they make their sales offer at the end of a content funnel. I've never had a bad reaction for my own services, either. That doesn't mean bad reactions can't happen — selling is both art and science, and you *can* get it wrong, but if you are putting your customers first then you can feel confident that you'll usually get a good response.

If need be, practice your sales offers. Get a friend or colleague on the phone, or however you will be making pitches to customers, and practice on them. It's worth the awkwardness and will pay a huge ROI on the time and energy you spend on it. Ideally, your practice partner will actually fit your primary customer profile. Give them your onboarding material to read first, so that they come to the practice sales situation with all the same knowledge your real prospects will have. Go through the process of the onboarding event — whether it's a webinar, demo or call — and then transition into your sales offer.

Practice moving the conversation from the free content to the sales offer. Practice your positioning, and how you talk about the offer. Practice the language that works best to communicate all the benefits of the offer, and practice how to overcome objections by encouraging your partner to come up with as many as they can, based on what you've already discussed. Finally, find out from them what questions went unanswered for them during the process, what objections they kept to themselves, and what would have made them commit to the sale that you didn't address. Try to get a real-world interaction that will emulate the sales process for you, so that when you do it with real prospects, you're in familiar territory.

Never pass up the opportunity to make a sale. If you have someone on a call, or in some kind of interaction with you, do not put it off. Do not say to yourself *"I'll just send them an email that closes them after this"* or *'they'll tell me if they want to go ahead with something"*. No you won't, and no they won't. Unless you have explicitly promised not to sell them anything, always be selling.

(The only time you should ever promise not to sell during an interaction is when you need something from the prospect other than the sale, like early market feedback. Otherwise, avoid making promises that will prevent you making money.)

Be as generous and fully present as you can possibly be during the sales process. Answer every question honestly and with your full attention. Dig into their doubts, invite them to hit you with their best shot — make them understand that you *really* care about their situation and helping them to find the right solution. Before they get off the call, get a yes or no answer from the prospect. Just ask: *"Are you ready to go ahead?"* No maybes, or let-me-think-about-its. Yes or no. If they push back on you, simply say that you want to get a specific answer from them so you know how to move forward with them. It might sound aggressive, but when positioned correctly, this is a powerful method to make sure that all the content you've produced so far actually does the job and makes people convert.

The Money Is In The Follow-Up

This is the most important principle you can learn in marketing. It's rare that a visitor will convert on their first visit to your site, or that even a warm prospect will convert at their first point of contact with you. Of course, if your initial onboarding funnel does a great job of orienting them into your business and demonstrating your value, you might have a pretty good conversion rate right out of the gate. But for most companies (particularly those making high price-point offers) getting the conversion can take a few interactions. People want to get to know the way you approach the industry, that you're a trustworthy and legitimate company, and that there are other people who have successfully done business with you.

Now, assuming that your prospects have gone through each part of the ecosystem, they should know, like and trust you. They should understand the benefits of what you're offering, and they should understand your perspective on the industry. If they haven't bought from you yet, then it's time to bring a follow-up system to life so that all your hard work helps get them past the tipping point, rather than indefinitely hovering around it.

If someone says no when you make your sales offer, here's what you do. You tell them that you are going to send them a recap of your conversation, so that they can reply with any questions that come to them afterwards, and that you're going to follow up with them in a few weeks (and make sure it goes on your calendar to do so). When you follow up with them as promised, you'll often find that they have made no progress towards their stated goals. This is where you can restate their exact motivation for speaking with you, and highlight how you can help them: *"Here's the offer I made you last time. Here's the way I can make it even better for you, so you can stop wasting time and start seeing the progress you need: [insert offer here of a discount, done-for-you element, additional features, bonuses etc]."*

Something I've seen used to great effect at this stage is inviting them to get back on the phone with you *and* to bring their business partner along for the conversation. This way, you can answer any more questions, speak directly to the problems they've already shared with you, reinforce why you're a great fit for their business, and get them working together to make a buying decision on the spot.

Until someone specifically says, *"No. I don't want what you're offering, and I don't want to talk to you about it anymore"*, you can keep following up. It doesn't have to be aggressive or pushy — you can make it a powerful demonstration of free, useful value — but you should keep at it. Research from Salesforce shows that it can take a business six to eight interactions with a customer before they will see a conversion,[4] so until you get a hard no, they're still a lead. People take time to make buying decisions. Maybe their industry moves slowly, maybe their business moves slowly, maybe they have shareholders or a board they have to justify decisions to… sometimes you need to be a little patient.

Alternately, if you would rather automate your follow-up, you can build out two email funnels to do all this work for you: one funnel for people who converted,

---

[4]

https://www.salesforce.com/blog/2015/04/takes-6-8-touches-generate-viable-sales-lead-heres-why-gp.html and one for people who have not converted yet, using the same process you used to build your onboarding email funnel. The funnel for people who do convert should include welcome material, next steps for them to get started with you, and bonus content. For people who have not converted yet, provide more educational, useful content, and keep inviting them to conversion opportunities.

Action Steps for Chapter Six:

Here's the checklist to use every time you want to create powerful, high-converting, profitable content:

- Make your content timely and actionable.
Timely doesn't always have to mean that it's about some current news event (though you should always aim to capitalize on those events): it can be timely for where customers are at in the buying cycle, it can be seasonal, or it can be evergreen and always relevant.

- Make the content very valuable.
It should present educational, fresh information that the customer is not going to get elsewhere. Even if it's not new material, make sure you present it with a new angle or a better way of looking at it. Every piece of content you produce should give the customer something new to think about or act on, and set you apart from the competition as a knowledgeable, trustworthy authority.

- Keep the message focused on the customer.
It's not about you – it's always about them. Focus on what fears or problems they need to overcome, what information they need to succeed, and the steps

they can take to get there. Frame everything, even if it's about you or your products, in terms of what it will do for them.

- Stick to a single message for each piece of content.

In the $10,000 Case Study example earlier in the book, the message was *'Supplement stuffing is bad, because consumers have a right to know what they're getting'*. This is a simple, focused message, whereas *'Supplement stuffing is bad because consumers have a right to know what they're getting, corporations are evil... buy our supplements instead'* would have created confusion about the purpose of the post and would have prevented people from taking the desired action – which was voting with their wallets.

- Don't go for the hard sell.

Most people are not going to buy from you the first time they come across your business – they don't know you or trust you yet (you can think of it like dating... you wouldn't marry someone you've only been on one date with. I hope). It's much more effective in this situation to use the soft sell approach. Let people know where they can find your products if they're interested, and leave it at that. This strategy is surprisingly powerful (as that $10,000 week proved).

- Promote, promote, promote!

If you don't promote your content, you may as well not make it at all. People need to see it where they are at: Facebook, Twitter, Instagram, Reddit, their inbox, their podcast updates... put it EVERYWHERE. And don't just do it once. Create a promotional calendar so that your content gets bumped regularly in slightly different ways to make sure it's reaching new audiences all the time. You can use a similar spreadsheet to the one you use to plan your quarterly content, adjusted to focus on the message to be shared across each platform for each post.

- Make sure you're collecting their email addresses.

This is critical. If you are driving lots of traffic to your content, but not collecting a way to connect with them, again, you might as well not have made it. The whole point of making content is to get people to engage with your business: email pop-ups and opt-in offers are a vital part of doing this. Remember: most people won't buy from you the first time, so you need a way to be in regular contact with them, so they learn to trust you enough to eventually buy what you're offering.

Creating your content according to this checklist will give you strong advantage in your marketplace and will increase the amount of revenue you see from your content.

Chapter Seven: Creating Your Content Assets

Content assets are long-form pieces of content that you can use to attract high-end clients, by demonstrating that you are an authority, and that you have an uncommon depth of knowledge in your industry. Sharing your expertise in a generous, transparent way like this is a powerful way to get your business in front of big clients who could change the game for you. In your content asset, you really pull back the curtain on your expertise, writing the playbook on how your clients could implement your custom strategies to solve their problems.

It sounds like giving away your secret sauce, but in reality, people just want to taste the sauce and know how you make it, rather than making the sauce themselves. The ingredients for Sriracha Hot Sauce are listed in detail on Wikipedia, but no one wants to make it themselves. They want to buy that bottle with the rooster on it and have it ready to go without having to go find all the specialty grocers, get the right balance of ingredients and then sweat it out in the kitchen themselves. It's the same with your process: people are curious about the details, but they really just want the result without having to do the work themselves.

ViperChill is just one business that provides a great example of this. The owner, Glen Allsopp, regularly produces incredibly valuable long-form content about SEO on his blog. He doesn't withhold any key information, or force you to opt in to get this content. He shares everything that's been working for his selection of SEO-drive niche websites, big upcoming opportunities in the industry, as well as transparent updates about the progress of his business. Far from costing him work, Glen gets to be totally selective about his client roster — his expertise and generosity show that he's the best in the business, and so the best in *other* businesses line up to work with him.

The big win, of course, is that pulling back the curtain like this makes you look like a giant. It implies that it doesn't matter to you if people do it themselves, or even if your competitors steal your system — your business is so robust and you have so much confidence in your process that you can easily afford for that to happen. It's an attractive attitude to clients who want to work with the best in the field.

The most common content assets used in B2B businesses are books and training courses. Any large piece of content you create that will hold its value and separate you from the market is a content asset. I'm going to use books as my key example throughout this section, as that's what I specialize in, but all this information applies just as well to training courses and other long-form assets.

If you want create authority for your business, create a steady flow of leads, to charge more than market standards, and to win more business without having to do any extra prospecting, then writing a book is unparalleled. But many people shy away from it:

- It takes work and it takes time
- It's not particularly innovative, and can't be given some proprietary name
- It requires giving away the farm / secret sauce, which many businesses don't want to do
- It's not a ground-breaking idea, but it could transform your business

Maybe you've already thought about it. Even though we live in the age of constant content, blog posts and podcasts are flimsy by comparison to a book or course. Anyone can bang out a few hundred words and press publish, or record their thoughts into their iPhone and upload it for listeners. Only the experts write books.

◆ ◆ ◆

Creating a content asset and building a strategy around it is not the right move for all businesses. Ecommerce companies, for example, are generally better served by recurring content. Businesses with low price-point products also do better with recurring content — there's a much lower barrier to purchase among the audience and creating a long-form asset may be overkill. But if your business sells high-ticket items or services, then a content asset is a powerful demonstration of authority and credibility. It can shortcut the process of winning trust and confidence from potential clients, and is an incomparable differentiator from your competitors.

Content assets should be used as an upgrade to your recurring content. While recurring content is fantastic — it gets you in front of a wide audience and helps you become an authority — having a content asset puts you head and shoulders above the rest of the businesses in your market. It shows that you are serious about your industry (you've got to be serious to write a book), that you are a real authority with real resources and expertise behind you, and it functions as a calling card. Building a content asset sets you apart from your competitors in a way that no other exercise can: short of a massive windfall event or paying for the Tim Ferriss Effect,[5] there's no way of building niche authority faster than writing a book or running a course.

---

[5] https://medium.com/@kevinslavelle/the-tim-ferriss-effect-7d3dff9c63dc#.y7i9fhlwj

Now, I'm not going to lie to you: It requires a massive effort to build this kind of content asset. If you are running your own business, finding the time to write every day is going to be tough — particularly to get to the kind of word count that makes publishing a book worthwhile. And once you decide to write a book, speed to market becomes important, so that you're not beaten to the punch by a competitor with the same idea.

All the people for whom I've ghostwritten books have met with this exact problem: they have too much to do in their businesses to make real progress on their book each day. They realize that if it's going to happen, someone else needs to take the lead. Where they can produce 300 or 500 words a day, a good professional writer can produce 3000 to 5000 words a day… and when you're writing a book with a 40,000 or 50,000 word count, the difference in timeline is massive.

What usually decides it for them, though, is that the book needs to be marketed *at the same time* it is being written. If you are going to create real momentum for your business with your book, it needs to launch to fanfare and blanket coverage where your primary customers are going to see it (not to launch to crickets and then slowly build up a following over time). The business owner has the connections and positioning to make that happen, but they can't do that and write the damn thing at the same time. They hand the legwork off to me, and then focus instead on getting it in front of the right people. Even if you have a dedicated audience who will be supportive, you want to be seeding their interest, getting early purchasing commitments from them, and having them commit to sharing it for you when the time comes.

That element — getting it in front of the right people — is the most critical part of producing a content asset. You want to use it to attract higher value customers, and as a way to 'rack the shotgun' to get the attention of people who are serious about solving the problem you specialize in. The people who are willing to read a book about your solution are often going to be the same people who are willing to pay an expert to take care of it for them — when you're thinking about creating an asset like this, you need to to think of it with your future sales system in mind.

How to Start Creating Your Content Asset

Step One: Clarify Your Concept
Regardless of whether you decide to produce your content asset yourself, or outsource it to someone like me, you need to start with a very clear concept in mind.

A client whose book I worked on had a well-defined concept for his content asset: teaching insurance agents how to transition their in-person business model over to an online business model, including all the practical steps they would need to make it happen.

Another client wanted to write a book to teach retail brands how to get involved in online retail, with all the intricate details of getting a store established on the big retail platforms and how to then expand into international retail territories.

For this book, my concept was:

"Content that converts: teaching entrepreneurial B2B business owners about how to use content marketing in their businesses, so that they can consistently get more leads and convert more of those leads into customers with high lifetime values."

Step Two: Build Your Outline

So, you've got a clear idea about what your content asset is going to deliver, and to whom you will be speaking. Once you've got your topic nailed down (and you should be able to communicate the key message in a sentence or two), you want to build an outline. This is a critical part of creating your content asset, regardless of whether it's a book or course. You must know what you're going to talk about, before you start talking about it. Without a very detailed roadmap, you will get hopelessly lost and discouraged, and the asset will never get finished. Creating a robust outline is the foundation of creating a content asset that will address all the elements that a customer needs in order to convert.

Your outline is going to be your guiding light through the entire asset creation process. You'll be able to ensure that you include all the important information around your concept, without having to worry about whether you've missed something important. You'll be able to see where you're up to at all times, how much work is left to go, and where things need to be rearranged to make the most sense for the reader. Your outline will also be a living document — it will grow and change over time as your ideas emerge and the asset takes shape, so give yourself plenty of time to build this out, and don't stress out if you realize that the outline needs to be revised once you start work.

You'll give yourself a running start if you include as much detail in the outline as you possibly can. Write down every point you can think of, and group similar points together to form the structure of chapters. I recommended a chapter count of seven, 12, 15 or 21 chapters, depending on the depth and style of the book — these are numbers most people are conditioned to seeing in books and you want to create a sense of order and familiarity for your readers right from the start. The more detail you have in your outline, the easier it will be for you to extract all the important knowledge from your head and get it onto the page: your points should be condensed enough that you can simply flow from writing everything you know about one point, to everything you know about the next point. You can see my outline for this book on the Resources page, at laurahanly.com/ctc-resources.

Step Three: How to Build Out the Content

> *"I can see no way out but through."*
> — *Robert Frost*

There's no point sugarcoating it — this is the point where you have to put your butt in a chair, turn off your internet, and write through each of the points in your outline. Mr Frost has got it nailed here. You just have to go through the process, but I've spoken to many, many would-be authors who just can't get past this. The thought of trying to write 40,000 words just crushes them, and they end up rooted to the spot, facing down the project that is both their biggest opportunity and biggest roadblock.

Fortunately, it doesn't have to be the horrible ordeal that many entrepreneurs and business owners think it is going to be, and I can guarantee this, because

I've used the exact process I'm about to share with you to write six books this year. You can use this process to create any kind of content, whether it's blog posts, sales copy or your book, though it works particularly well for more long-form content, because it's much, much faster than trying to write everything down piece by piece.

Once you've got your outline built, you're going to record yourself talking through everything you know about each of the points you've got listed. The way I go about this with clients is to pick one to two chapters that we will work through per recording session, and then I ask them all about each point listed in each of those selected chapters. The client tells me everything they know, and I act as the advocate for the reader — asking questions to clarify meaning, uncover context and deeper information, and get direction about what to do with this information they're sharing. We record these conversations, and then I go away and transcribe it, adding in additional resources and content they've provided to me as I go.

You can use the exact same process if you are working on your own. You just need to be conscientious that the reader doesn't have the luxury of asking you questions as they go, so you need to make sure you don't assume they know particular background information or that they understand the jargon or logical leaps you're making as you talk through it all.

I recommend keeping your recording sessions to an hour or so, or to two chapters at a time. It's surprisingly tiring to verbalize all the information you've accumulated over years of work — every point you make requires explanation and exploration to make complete sense. That said, you can produce all the 'raw' material for the book in a week or two using this system, and then it's just a matter of transcribing it and adding extra resources and content as necessary. You can feasibly have a first draft completed within four to six weeks if you're working with a good writer, or eight to ten weeks working on your own (working on your own could take less time if you use a transcription service to convert your recorded material into writing, though I would recommend transcribing it yourself, as listening to yourself speak will highlight where you need to add extra content or detail — this doesn't happen so much when you're reading something that's already 'complete').

This system allows you to communicate all your unique insight, expertise and perspective, in your unique voice, without requiring some unbearable (or unfeasible) time commitment. The transcription will take the longest, because you have to wrangle the stream of speech into a format that works for a book, and you'll always find areas that need to be filled out, improved or rearranged.

Most business owners can clearly see the value of having a book, but they don't want to spend weeks (or months, once they factor in running their business) fleshing it out. Instead, they spend six or seven hours in conversation with me over a week or two, field a few more questions over email, and then a month or so later I surface with their words and expertise in the form of a completed draft, ready to work with them on final edits and marketing. (If this is an option you would like to explore for your own content assets, send an email to laura@laurahanly.com, and I'll be in touch to arrange a discovery call.)

However, if you prefer to create your long-form asset yourself, set yourself a schedule to get all your recordings done, so that you start making real, tangible progress quickly. An hour every two days seems to be a good rate of production for most people — it's enough time to make a big dent in the raw material, but not so much that your other responsibilities grind to a halt. The best way to do it is to grab your phone and headset, write down the chapter topics and all the points to cover, and then head out for a walk as you record yourself on your phone's voice recording software. Of course, you can do it sitting at your desk if you prefer, but it can be uncomfortable to be sitting around talking to yourself within earshot of other people!

Pro tip: as soon as you get back, upload your recording to Dropbox or whatever cloud storage you use. You never know when your phone is going to dropped, lost or drowned, and that's bad enough without losing all your recordings!

If you really want to speed up your rate of production, you can do transcriptions on the days you're not recording. Pick a word count you'd like to get through for each day, and gradually work through your recordings whenever you have the time. For example, you might decide on 1000 words per day — depending on how fast you speak, this is usually going to be between eight and 12 minutes of recorded content, or maybe one or two points of the chapter you're working through. Knowing all this, then, you can project roughly how long it will take you to produce the draft, which enables you to plan marketing and launch events accordingly.

Once you've processed all the recordings, you need to go through an editing process (and this is true for any content asset — books, courses and blog posts all need some sort of editing). I recommend asking two or three people who are familiar with the content to be early readers for you. They should be looking out for a) typos and grammar mistakes and b) structural issues (missing information, confusing layout etc). Don't give it to people who don't want to know about your concept, or who are not going to be able to see the big picture of what you're trying to achieve.

IMPORTANT: DO NOT GIVE YOUR READERS ACCESS TO YOUR ORIGINAL DOCUMENTS. Only you (and your ghostwriter if you have one) should be able to access the actual draft. _Make a copy_ of the original draft that your early readers can comment on — not edit directly — so that you can track their suggestions. Otherwise you won't know what changes have been made, and you end up with a total mess throughout this very important asset.

Give them two weeks (or whatever timeline works for your schedule), and then go through and implement all the edits and suggestions that you think are appropriate when held up to the concept of the book. Sometimes, you will get well-meaning but wrong suggestions, which you should ignore, and other times you'll get strokes of genius that _must_ be included, so make sure you've got a week or two to work through all the feedback and implement what you want before you send the asset off for formatting and production. Have a professional do the formatting and creative design for you, so that you get a highly polished, attractive and professional final product. This is the last milestone — making the presentation match the quality of the content, so that you can prepare to leverage the asset into a new sales channel for your business, and it's the time when you have to trust the asset into the hands of design professionals.

Step Four: Leveraging the Asset
'Leveraging the asset' sounds a bit like something out of a Jason Bourne film, and if you're a content nerd like yours truly, it's every bit as exciting. This is the process of creating a groundswell around the asset you've created, building a following and real, dollars-in-the-bank engagement from customers.

As I mentioned earlier, you want to start marketing the asset at the same time that it's being created. Don't wait until it's all finished to start promoting it to potential customers and publicity partners. Internal formatting and cover design can take a few weeks once the final draft is completed, so use that time to line up guest posts, podcast interviews, giveaways, and launch events, as well as advertising and email marketing to build up to the launch date.

Private Facebook Group:

Ideally, you would start a private Facebook group while you're still working on the draft so that you can get early buy-in from people who fit your primary customer profile, and get them to help you promote it when the time comes. You also want people who are interested and knowledgeable about the content you're covering, and can be trusted to give you honest feedback, to ask thought-provoking questions, to act as early readers to make sure it's as good as can be, and support you getting it out into the world. Having this early involvement gives people a sense of ownership in the book, so they will be more likely to help promote and share it with the right people at the time of publication.

Some things to consider here:

- You need a very specific purpose and direction for the Facebook group, so that it's valuable to everyone involved, rather than becoming just another thing that sucks up their time (and yours). Make sure you're clear about how you will use it and what its value will be before you set anything up.

- Can you commit to running a Facebook group? Updating it every day with interesting additional information, and sharing your process and expertise in real time?
- Are you comfortable documenting your progress and sharing content that might not be as polished or perfect as it will be once it's published?
- Can you handle getting real-time feedback (particularly if it's negative or uncomfortable) and working that into the fabric of the book?
- Are you willing to include people in the key decisions around the book, including choosing the title, cover design, and adjusting the structure and content as necessary?

If you can answer 'yes' to all those questions, then it's a powerful tool to have in your arsenal. A Facebook group will grow in value over time, and continue to be a resource once the book is published. Taylor Pearson used this strategy for The End of Jobs, as did Dan Norris with The 7-Day Startup. Both of those groups grew massively after the publication of the book, and has provided ongoing opportunities and value to the authors and their communities. Don't think of this as just another annoying social media thing you have to do — Dan set up a 'Pro' version of The 7-Day Startup group, where people pay to play and get additional content and access. It can be a legitimate revenue stream for the business if you cultivate it carefully from the beginning.

Podcasts and Guest Posts:

Once the draft is finished, you'll have that lag time of a few weeks while all the formatting and publication preparation is happening. During this time, you want to be lining up podcast interviews and guest posts that will go live around the publication date. At this stage, pick a few low-hanging fruit — podcasts that are very specific to your industry, or where you can get an introduction (of course, making sure they're actually relevant). Send the host a completed draft with a few recommendations about chapters or pages you think they would find interesting, as well as a few potential talking points that would be valuable for their listeners.

Do the same with blogs for which you could contribute guest posts. Having a few adapted sample chapters featured on the big blogs in your industry is a powerful way to get widespread, targeted coverage. This can drastically increase the amount of engagement the book gets around the launch period, and the coverage can be leveraged into bigger and bigger opportunities as the project gains momentum.

Blurbs, Reviews and Testimonials:

Hopefully over the course of your professional development, you've been investing in building your network and building up a nice fat bank of goodwill amongst your connections. If you've been helpful and generous, without asking much of people around you, now is the moment to dip into that resource. Ask for introductions to podcast hosts and successful bloggers and high-profile people in your industry. Ask for a promotion on social media or to an email list, or ask for a blurb or testimonial to include in the book to boost your social proof. Your network is not an endless well, so don't drain it, but provided you have good relationships, ask for help and be willing to provide value in return.

You should be collecting any positive feedback you get from early readers or your media placements so that you can use it to promote the book across your platforms. Make sure you get permission, but once you've got it, plaster your good reviews everywhere. If you don't have any reviews to begin with, you can use past feedback from customers about you as an expert instead. Reviews and testimonials from relevant sources are very important for building credibility and interest, and can help overcome any resistance a potential reader has to picking up the book.

Thunderclap Campaign:

Thunderclap is a mass social media campaign coordinator. You can create a standardized message for multiple platforms and have all your Facebook group members, friends and colleagues share it on their accounts around the same time. This gives you a very wide spread of coverage, and can help get the book in front of a much greater audience than it would have reached otherwise. I'd recommend reaching out to all your friends in the business space, even if they're not directly connected to your industry, to help with this. Contact them a few weeks in advance, and give them the option to join the Facebook group so they can get a feel for what the book is about, and so they will feel comfortable promoting it to their network. You never know who you're just a few degrees of separation from, so this additional reach can be very powerful.

Amazon Reviews:

When the book is released, list it for free on Amazon for the first week or so. Use this free period to get as many people as possible to download it, and leave to you good reviews. You can add an element of urgency to this process by letting people know that the price will be going up in a few days. This is the key to gaining long-term momentum with the book, particularly if you plan to use it as a revenue stream — you want to get as many downloads and good reviews as you can. Ideally you would list the book in a relevant category where you have a chance of hitting bestseller status, so that all the downloads and reviews result in that coveted 'bestseller' tag that you can use for additional credibility and authority. If that does happen, make sure you get in contact with some of the bigger players in the industry that you haven't been in contact with yet. Send them the podcasts or guest posts you've done already, along with the bestseller information, to let them know you'd be a good fit for their platform. Keep the coverage rolling as long as you can!

Launch Party and Promotions:

You've been working your butt off to get this thing done — time to party! Throw a launch party to celebrate, and use it as an opportunity to get face to face with influential people who can help expand the reach of the book. Invite everyone who has helped you get it done, and anyone who can help you leverage it. Order some physical copies of the book, get some wine and nice food, and take a moment to reflect on the work you've done and what an achievement publishing a book is. This shouldn't be a pitch-fest or a hard marketing event, but it will produce some natural opportunities to move the asset forward. At the same time, use it to create some cool social media coverage, and run a competition to win a copy of the book, or (if you want to go really big) get a consult, an in-person meeting or a surprise bonus pack.

Using Your Content Asset In The Niche Marketing Sales Process

Once your book or asset is out in the world, you've successfully launched (and taken a minute to recover), you can start using the asset as the client acquisition tool it was originally designed to be.

If you have a high-end service with a long sales cycle, this is about to be your secret weapon. As soon as you get a lead, send them a copy of the book, with a note directing them to a section that will be immediately useful to them. This is a seamless way to show that you're a real expert, and that you're a smooth operator who knows what they need and how to get them results.

I first heard of this sales technique when I was studying up on a marketing agency based in Washington state. This agency picked a professional niche where profit margins were high and speed of customer acquisition was critical to success, and so they created a highly specific offer, tailored just to that market.

They started out by producing a great blog with high-quality content, and consistently invited people to join their mailing list. After a while, they realized that while this front-end content was bringing qualified leads to them, they needed a content asset with some real 'wow factor' to get their high-end prospects across the line. With that in mind, they wrote a book, ranked it on Amazon, and used it as a tool to create that 'conversion moment' in a more tangible way.

They promoted the book to their email list (which was healthy and engaged, thanks to all the quality blog content), ran Facebook ads to the book's landing page, and sent out physical copies to potential customers in their area. Every book that was dispatched came with a strong call to action, inviting the prospect to schedule a consult once they'd read the book and decided whether they were interested.

Once they were on the call, the agency would answer all their questions, outline some strategies, and provide insights on things that the prospect could implement immediately. Finally, the agency would ask if the prospect would like to engage their services. If the prospect said yes, they would process the sale right there on the phone. If the prospect didn't want to make a decision right then, they would say *"No problem. We'll mark you down as a no for now, and follow up with you in a few months."*

This would provoke one of two responses. *"Well, it's not that I'm saying no…"* which would open up the conversation about why they were stalling and get to the core of the real objection so they could move forward, or they would say *"Okay, that sounds great."* End of story. Either way, the agency got a win and capitalized on the opportunity their content asset had created for them. Within three months of implementing this book-and-call strategy, they added over $20,000 in monthly recurring revenue to their business. At the time of writing this book, they had been using this strategy for about 18 months, and their total annual revenue had nearly tripled.

To make this happen in your own business, your sales process needs to be as consistent with the rest of the customer's experience as it can possibly be. You don't want a customer to ever feel that they're suddenly talking to a different person or a different business when they get to the point of being made this offer. If your language suddenly becomes stiff and formal, or infomercial-salesy, they're going to find that jarring and you'll lose them. If the branding and formatting of a sales page is very different to all the material they've seen prior, they're going to find that jarring and you'll lose them. If you put the hard sell on them, when to this point it's been very casual, they'll find that jarring and again, you'll lose them.

I cannot emphasize this enough: creating a consistent customer experience is absolutely critical to your conversions. A 2014 McKinsey study[6] found that there was a direct correlation between consistency throughout the customer journey and the total amount of revenue the business will see from them:

6

http://www.mckinsey.com/industries/retail/our-insights/the-three-cs-of-customer-satisfaction-consistency-consistency-consistency

"For companies wanting to improve the customer experience as a means of increasing revenue and reducing costs, executing on customer journeys leads to the best outcomes. We found that a company's performance on journeys is 35 percent more predictive of customer satisfaction and 32 percent more predictive of customer churn than performance on individual touchpoints."

Make sure your sales content and process uses the same language, same visual elements, and same positioning as all your previous content to ensure the customer stays in a positive frame of mind throughout.

When they agree to make the sale, simply take it in stride and move them on to the next step. Keep it cool, and make sure you get them moving forward — just as you saw earlier in the funnel, you should never leave them hanging, wondering about what to do next. Whether that's processing the sale over the phone or sending them a payment link or invoice with a deadline, make sure they understand what they need to do next, and what they can expect from you.

An important thing to include when you are developing your sales pitch is a question about the specific problem they are trying to solve in their business. Try to found out what the exact issue is, and why are they motivated to talk to you about it. This gives you a precise insight into what *they* think the problem or need is, and it will often turn out to be something quite different to what *you* would have otherwise assumed. If you get their exact words down when you speak to them, you can put it in your follow-up email and restate the problem back to them whenever you have a conversation. This reinforces that you are paying attention and know how to solve this particular issue, and will make sure that when they decide to act, yours will be the company they choose. It's also a powerful tool to leverage later on if they decide not to take you up on your initial sales offer, because you can cite it the next time you make contact.

Action Steps for Chapter Seven:

1. Map out how a long-form content asset could be put to use in your business. Would a book or training course work better? Who would it be targeted at? How would you market it?

2. Create a rough outline: 12 topics that could become chapters or modules, and work out how long it would take you to produce this content.

3. Cross-reference it with your calendar for the next six months — when would be the ideal time to launch this asset? If you decide to have someone help you with it, when would you need to start moving to make sure it launches at the ideal time?

Chapter Eight: Distributing Your Content with Email Marketing

Creating a content strategy that converts — whether a recurring strategy or an asset-driven one — relies on having a consistent stream of fresh eyes seeing your content. Your content might be the most incredible resource ever created for your industry, but if no one sees it, you'll never make a cent from it. It's the old philosophical question: if a tree falls in the forest and no one is around to hear it, does it make a sound?

This is not the place to explore the nature of observation and reality, but you can bet your bottom dollar that you have to proactively distribute your content if you want people to engage with it, become part of your audience, eventually convert on an offer, and potentially become a lifelong customer.

Email marketing is still one of the most powerful marketing strategies you can use to get the most out of your content. People have been lamenting for years that 'email is dead', but it's still the most direct way you can connect with your audience. It's the only medium that goes directly to them, and can be personalized down to their name, past purchases and specific interests. We'll go into specific campaign types shortly, but first let's cover a few best practice points.

Email Best Practices

Choosing an email provider
I personally use Active Campaign. I like its user interface and how easily you can customize your lists. Drip is another great option, and both of these are

ideal for small to mid-size companies who have big expansion plans. Ontraport and Infusionsoft are ideal if you're already big, or if you have a more complex offering with lots of moving parts. Mailchimp was popular for a long time, but their capabilities and value proposition have not kept up with their competitors (and you'll find a list of providers I recommend on the Resources page: laurahanly.com/ctc-resources/)

Send details

Make sure the 'from' name in all your email campaigns is actually something people will recognize and engage with. If you are the face of your brand, then the 'from' name should be *your* name, but if your brand isn't represented by one person, then just use the name of the business. It's familiar to your audience and will let them know who's showing up in their inbox.

Make sure, also, that the actual email address you're sending from is active. Do *not* use 'noreply@business.com'. Forcing people to respond to you through the contact form on your site or by submitting a support ticket is just going to alienate them — why do you get to email them, if they don't get to email you? Remember that it's a privilege to be able to communicate with customers directly, and that you need to be respectful of that relationship.

Subject line

David Ogilvy, perhaps the most famous advertiser who ever lived, said *"On the average, five times as many people read the headline as read the body copy. When you have written your headline, you have spent eighty cents out of your dollar."* In emails, this is your subject line. This is the single most important thing for you to get right in your email marketing.

Neil Patel, who built marketing software Crazy Egg, found that of all the variables in email marketing that he tested, the subject line tests yielded a 62% increase in performance, compared to 19% for the actual content, and 6% for both frequency and time of day.

People always ask me about the best time of day to send, how often to email their list, and whether they should put the whole piece of content in the body, or just have an excerpt linked back to their blog... but none of it matters if no opens the damn email! Your subject line is your ambassador and your biggest opportunity to engage people who are already interested in your business.

No pressure though.

Here are some general tips for writing good subject lines:

- Keep them short (preferably less than 50 characters).
- Mix them up and test what works. Avoid using the same style for every email.
- Ask questions, give hints or make an interesting claim.
- Don't go nuts on the hyperbole, exclamation points or promotional phrases (keep in mind that exclamation points can land you in the spam folder, too).
- Test, test, test. Your email platform should allow you to test headline variations, send times and body content, so make use of this with each campaign until you begin to see patterns emerge.
- Don't be misleading. Nothing annoys customers more than a bait and switch.
- Use urgency carefully. It's powerful but can wear thin if it's used too much.

- Did I mention testing? Test regularly! The results will change over time.

Pre-header

This is the line that shows up in your customer's inbox, next to the subject line. If you remove it from your email template, the first line of your email will show up, but if you choose to keep it, make sure you're actually using it effectively — you can think of it as a continuation of the subject line.

A good option is to give a hint or snippet of what's going to be in the body, but whatever you do, make sure it's not *'Having trouble viewing this email? Click here to open in your browser.'* No one has trouble viewing their emails and even if they do, it's very unlikely that they're going to be bothered to open it in their browser. Make this real estate work for you, instead of setting you back.

Body design

The content that actually goes into the body of the email depends largely on the kind of business and offering you have. John McIntyre, who runs an email marketing service called ReEngager, has this to say:

"If your email is 100% text with no branding elements whatsoever, it will probably get marked as spam because people won't know immediately who the email is from. If you go too heavy on the fancy design elements – like beautiful images, animated GIFs, and crazy layouts – your email is more likely to be picked up by email algorithms and sent to the promotions tab or folder. You have to strike a balance: simple enough that your email feels at least somewhat personal, fancy enough that it gets attention without triggering the promotions tab (or worse, the spam folder)."

Copy and messaging

By now, you should have a clear grasp on the language and messaging your market segment responds to best. All the copy that goes into your emails — whether they are autoresponders or one-off broadcasts — should reflect that messaging and be very consistent. The reader should feel like they're getting emails from the same person every time, and that those emails have a clear purpose.

Timing

As I mentioned earlier, the timing of when you send your emails has less impact on email performance than various other factors. If you're sending valuable information, you should see good engagement no matter when you hit send. Of course, it's worth optimizing this once you've got the other variables nailed down, so run some tests over time to see which send times and days perform best.

For example, a client of mine who had a software business found that Saturday morning at 9am was the best time to send, which surprised me — who is checking their emails at that time?! Software guys, apparently. A consultant I worked with got great opens at 2pm on a Wednesday… maybe his audience had gotten through their biggest tasks for the week and were catching up on their emails around that time. There's no one-size-fits-all here, so work out what's right for your business.

The timing element that is most important is actually your frequency. Again, it depends on your business and your email list. For some businesses, emailing every day with short-form content performs really well, but for others a daily email would be a disaster. For many businesses, a weekly email is a safe bet (and this is where I would recommend starting when promoting your content), though in your industry it might be every two weeks, or even once a month, again depending on your customer profile and your offerings.

Mobile optimization

There's been a big shift to mobile devices in just a few years, and for most businesses, mobile traffic now accounts for around 50% of their engagement, both on websites and via email. You want to make sure your emails are mobile optimized (and most providers will have a check-box option that does this automatically for you). If you're including images in the body content, make sure that the message of the email still works if the image doesn't show up for mobile users — if the image contains critical information, many of your mobile users won't see it, as images often don't display in mobile email apps.

Email Campaigns

There are three key types of email campaigns that you can put to use in your business. Each of these serves a specific purpose: first, to engage your audience immediately and let them know you'll be communicating with them; second, to help them get to and trust you and your business; and third, to make them relevant, timely sales offers.

1. Welcome

Most people expect some sort of welcome email when they sign up to your list. Don't let them down! A welcome email is a great way to engage them from the get-go, and to set their expectations that you will be making regular contact and offers. Use this email to introduce your company, how you're differentiated from your market, and to give them something valuable (either a gift or access to a resource). I'd recommend a welcome sequence of two to three emails that indoctrinates the new subscriber to your brand, gives them something cool, has them engage on any appropriate social media platforms, and then feeds them into your lead nurture campaigns.

2. Lead Nurture

There are two types of lead nurture: autoresponder sequences made up of five or six emails that walk them through specific information (which is a good way to put older content to use) or broadcast campaigns, where you update them each week with the new content you've been producing. These emails are your opportunity to build up the bank of goodwill you have with your audience, by sharing educational material, entertaining stories, or interesting industry news. These should be the bulk of the emails you send. In these emails, you're not trying to sell anything. You're just sharing good information that builds your credibility and authority, so that when the time comes, your audience will be receptive to your offers.

3. Offers

The whole point of this entire book is to use your content to create opportunities to make sales offers. This is where that opportunity lies. It's very easy: you decide what you're going to offer, write an email, and send it out. That's the whole process, which you rinse and repeat, rinse and repeat. Make offers to new subscribers, make offers to old subscribers, make offers to people who have bought from you once or 50 times. Make strategic offers on strategic timelines: an offer every 10 or so emails is a good ratio. This keeps that bank of goodwill high, so that when you dip into it by asking the customer for something — which is what happens when you make an offer — they don't mind and might even be excited about it.

A Caveat...

A key aspect of developing a content marketing strategy that converts customers over the long term — creating a sustainable, profitable relationship that lasts for years and years — is to make far fewer goodwill withdrawals than you do deposits.

This is important to keep in mind at this point, as you start making your offers. Yes, you have to be aggressively acquiring new customers, and yes, you have to be making regular sales offers in order to get the conversions. But you don't want to push people so hard that they buy under all the pressure, and then vanish because they had such an unpleasant experience.

In order to make sure that your list stays healthy, you need to make sure you're constantly building goodwill with your customers. This is why you need to think of content marketing as an ecosystem. It's a cycle — you put good things in, and eventually good things will come out. People wear out if you are constantly hammering them with sales offers so make sure you take care to spread the offers out and give far, far more value than you hope to extract.

This is also why positioning and messaging are so important. If an offer has inconsistent messaging with the rest of the content the customer receives from you, it will be jarring and alienating for them and will *feel* like a bigger ask than it actually is. To make sure that your offers land as you intend them to — and convert as many customers as possible while maintaining that goodwill balance — make sure that you've been through the Action Steps in Chapter One, Two and Three.

To further care for your audience...

- Team up with other businesses offering great complementary products and to get your customers special deals. AppSumo does an amazing job of this and their customers are very loyal as a result.

- Give more value than you need to. When someone buys something from you, go above and beyond to let them know you appreciate them. If they buy a high-ticket service, send them a physical gift. If it's a product, send them a bonus. Make them delighted.

- Surprise your list with goodies beyond your normal content updates. Send long-form content bonuses, free downloads, or other valuable stuff they can immediately put into action.

- Get them access to cool events or people. Be their advocate and defender.

Take care of them better than anyone else. See them as real people who need love and nurturing just like the rest of us, and take responsibility for their growth and success.

Action Steps for Chapter Eight:

1. Assess your current email strategy:
   a. Do you have one? If so, is your platform the right option for you business, and have you tested your send details?
   b. Do you have a clear onboarding and offer sequence? If not, what would it take to get one up and running this quarter?
2. How can your email marketing be improved?
   a. How often are you making sales offers? Is your ratio of offers to goodwill healthy?

Chapter Nine: Distributing Your Content with SEO

This section was generously contributed by Nat Eliason, who used these content-specific SEO strategies to grow his traffic by 22,333%. He gets over 250,000 visits a month to his site thanks to this system.

Those numbers are not typos, so I'm confident you'll get some great results using Nat's method. It takes months — not days or weeks — but it's a very powerful strategy to create increasing visibility for your content, and if you would like to learn more about Nat's system, you can take his SEO course at becomeatechnicalmarketer.com.

These are all going to be processes you can do yourself, without being difficult or requiring an SEO expert to help you, or having to spend a lot of time acquiring backlinks.

◆ ◆ ◆

Ideally, you would use this system right from the outset of your content marketing strategy. If you've already got a strategy in place, then simply add these SEO steps into your process going forward.

There are three rules you should always keep in mind when thinking about SEO (and we're using Google as the example here, but they're true of any search engine);

- Rule 1: Google wants to people's questions, and to make money in the process

- Rule 2: Google knows more about how Google works than any SEO expert
- Rule 3: Google will fix any ranking 'trick' and may penalize you for using it once they spot it

If you take nothing else away from this section, remember that the key to organic SEO success is to focus on answering your customer's questions, better than anyone else.

Part One: Topic Research

When you're doing your Quarterly Content Planning, every idea for a post should be measured against a simple question: "Is this something people are searching for?" If the answer is yes, then you have an *existing topic* to write about. If the answer is no, then you can still write about it and get search traffic — you just have to approach it differently, because what you have in that case is a *new topic*.

Existing Topics

Existing topics have very high SEO potential — if people are searching for it, then you have a great opportunity to get a lot of traffic from writing about it. These are the articles where you might see hundreds or even thousands of visitors a day from writing a high-quality piece on the topic. Existing topics often have very high SEO competition, which is why it's good to have a mix of existing and new topics for your SEO strategy.

<u>New Topics</u>

These are topics that people aren't really searching for already, or that they might be searching for in a different way. These topics have lower SEO potential, and you're never going to get as much traffic from a new topic as you will for an existing topic (unless some 'viral' event happens). That said, there's also lower SEO competition, because no one else is trying to rank for those topics. The best way to create a new topic is to make up a word or term to describe what you're talking about. For example, Nat coined 'runway calculator' or 'savable income', and now gets significant amounts of traffic from promoting those terms. Creating your own lexicon or definitions makes it very easy to create a place for yourself in the rankings that will increase in value over time, as the concept or term spreads into general use (and having a well-promoted book or course will help with this significantly).

Part Two: Keyword Research

Keyword research is primarily useful for existing topics. If you have a new topic, there won't be much search volume, because you're going to be defining the term or concept as you go. For an existing topic, though, you will have a large volume of keywords to work through to find the right way to position your content.

Firstly, you want to come up with all the addressable keywords. These are all the variations someone might search for when they're looking for the topic you're covering. Next, it's time to assess the search volume for each keyword, assess the competition for each one, and then finally settle on the keyword you're going to target.

Step One: Addressable Keywords

In a spreadsheet, list out all the possible variations someone might be searching for around the topic you want to address. You might end up with a list of 10 to 20 keywords. In the next column, give each keyword a rating on how specific or broad it is — maybe a score of 1 is narrow and a score of 3 is broad. This is subjective, but it helps you to choose which ones to focus on. Very broad terms require long, very in-depth articles to get traction, while a narrow term will perform well without as much work. Tools like SEMRush can provide some early inspiration, as they let you look up the keywords your main competitors are ranking for.

Step Two: Assessing Keyword Volume

This is the process of working out how many people are searching Google for your selected keywords every month. Add this number in the next column of your spreadsheet, and then open up Google Keyword Planner (set up an account if you don't already have one). Go to the Tools section, and select 'Find new keywords and get search volume data.' Enter your first keyword and hit 'Get ideas'. It will then display the search volume over a period of time, but the number that matters is the average monthly searches. While you used to get the specific number of searches, Google adjusted this in 2016 to only show ranges to low-spend users (which you will be if you're not currently running any AdWords campaigns). You'll see ranges of 1–100, 100–1K, 1K–10K, 10K–100K, 100K–1M or 1M+. Grab that number and add it to your spreadsheet next to the keyword, then repeat the process for each of your keywords until you have a complete list. It's not as specific as you might like, but it will give you a ballpark idea of what you're dealing with.

Beneath the results for each keyword, you'll also see suggested keywords around this topic, along with their search volume ranges. This is a great resource for finding keywords that should be included in your marketing, and you should add them to your spreadsheet.

Step Three: Assessing Competition

This is where you work out how competitive each of the keywords are, and how easy it will be for you to rank them. This is subjective — it really depends on your perspective of what constitutes 'easy' and how much your site is already ranking. In the beginning, though, you really want to go after keywords that have low competition. Later on, once you've got the hang of it, you can go after higher competition keywords.

Back in the spreadsheet, add a final column for competition. You should note that competition has very little to do with the competition rating you will see in Google Keyword Planner — that only tells you how competitive it is to *buy ads* for that keyword. That's what the tool is for, but that's not how we're using it. The only way to work out the actual search competition is to go and search for the keywords and see what turns up. Make sure you search in an incognito window to get the actual results (in a regular window, Google will display content based on your previous browsing history, which will show skewed results).

For keywords that have a lot of content but not from any really big sites, you can list them as medium competition. For keywords that have a lot of content *and* big sites are contributing (like Wikipedia, Huffington Post, established news outlets etc), then the competition is high. If the results that show up don't specifically address the question being asked, or there's not much content around the keyword, then it's got low competition. And if the results show a lot of social media content — Reddit threads, Pinterest boards, Twitter or Facebook updates — that's a great sign that there's very little competition for the keyword, because Google will only pull content from social media platforms as a last resort.

Step Four: Picking Your Keyword

Once you've filled out each of the columns in your spreadsheet, you'll be ready to choose your keyword. To begin with, choose a keyword that has a monthly search volume of less than 10,000 and has low competition. At the beginning of your SEO strategy, you don't want to go after the high competition keywords. Instead, use a strategy called levelling up. Start with an easy keyword, and then over time, adjusting your article to address gradually harder keywords. Once an article is ranking for an easy keyword, you can change the title that will display in Google (this is different to the actual title that displays at the top of the article). If you're on WordPress, you can do this through the meta-title tag if you've got an SEO plug-in (like Yoast) running. If you scroll down to the bottom of the post in your editor, there should be a section called snippet editor or SEO title. As your article starts ranking for various keywords, you can update this title to each higher-competition keyword over time so that it shows up for gradually higher volume keywords.

Ideally, you would also choose keywords that are likely to bring you new business. For example, if someone searches for "accountant," they could be looking for any number of things — maybe they want to know what an accountant does, or how to become an accountant themselves. But someone searching for "hire accountant in Chicago" is looking for a very specific service.

These specific keywords are called longtail keywords and can pay off over the long term if you use them to rank for something you specifically offer.

Part Three: Writing The Post

Before you start writing the post, you should understand that there are five guiding principles of creating SEO-friendly content. If you can keep these points in mind, you'll find it much easier to get your articles to rank well.

Principle One: Answer The Question!

If you don't answer the question, Google won't rank you. Your answer should go deep on addressing the intent behind the search query — what are they *really* looking to find out? What's driving them to try to find this information? People are often looking for very specific information, so you need to shape the article around providing those details in an accessible way.

You want the article to provide *all* the information someone would want about this topic. Break up the formatting of the article so that people can easily find the exact element they're trying to uncover. Make it easy for them to skim the article and spot the part they're after.

Principle Two: Provide the Best Answer to the Question

It's not enough to just answer the question — you need to think about how all your competitors are answering this question. The best way to do this is to go and read the first three or four articles that show up for the keyword search, and assess what they did well and what they should have done better. Take notes as you go through so you can keep track of everything you want to touch on. For example, maybe one of the articles is extremely technical (and therefore alienating to an entry-level person), or is formatted really poorly and is difficult to read, or is just a list of steps to work through with no engaging story around it. Or on the positive side, maybe they have included powerful images, have created a really compelling narrative, or have included lots of additional resources to help the reader. Decide what needs to be included in your article to make it the best of the bunch.

Principle Three: Provide A Complete Answer

You'll often see content online that's a partial answer to a question — "look out for my next article to find out the rest of this process!" This work for clickbait traffic and getting social shares, but that is short lived. You're better off giving *all* the information in one really valuable article and improving its performance over time. Figure out everything that people want to know when they search for this term, and address all of it.

Principle Four: Make It Actionable

When someone reads your content, you want them to go away and act on it immediately — not to go back to Google to look for more information. If they go back to search again right away, it indicates to Google that your article did not do a good job of answering their question. If you can provide action items or a process then the piece will gradually perform better over time, as readers going away to action is a powerful indicator of high-quality content.

Principle Five: Overdeliver

Don't just go through the first four steps. Go above and beyond what the reader was expecting to get. Whether it's including additional resources, further reading, tools, a free ungated download… whatever it is, give them so much value that they can't help sticking around. This helps get the content shared organically, which also increases rankings over time.

Structuring the Article

There are a few important structural elements to factor into your articles to help them rank faster. Firstly, you want to make sure it's easily readable. This means having line breaks, images and subheadings that will help people actually go through the content rather than thinking *"Ugh, wall of text"* and going back to Google.

Don't stuff the article with the keyword you're using. Google penalizes keyword stuffing these days, and if you're writing good content about it, you're naturally going to use the keyword and variants of it, so don't waste your time (and your reader's goodwill) by wedging it in as often as you can. Just include it in the title and URL, and use it naturally a few times throughout the body.

You also want to include relevant links throughout the body of the article. This helps Google to work out how your article factors into the structure of the internet, and how it relates to the rest of your site. Try to link to high-authority sources — Wikipedia, research articles and so on. Links to a few high-quality sources helps performance much than lots of links to low-quality or unknown sources. Always try to link to authoritative sources.

You should include links to other content on your own site as is relevant, which will also help with follow-through traffic from SEO. If you have one article that is doing really well with SEO that contains lots of links to your other articles, it will pull the other articles up with it — people will click through to your other articles after reading the original one from the search results.

At the end of the article, have some action items or a list of steps for people to work through. This way, if people just want to know exactly how to do something, they'll be able to skim right through the body content and *still* get enough information to go and implement it, rather than going back to Google to find more information.

The final element is creating your headline. Besides providing the best, most comprehensive answer you can, this is the most important step in the whole process. If you don't have a good headline, no one will click on your article in the search results. The headline is what lets them know that they've found the right information, and helps them to choose which piece to click on first. Structure your headline around the specific keyword in an interesting way. Map out 10 or 20 potential headlines for each article until you hit on the one that's the most interesting and the most informative.

Part Four: Promoting the Article

Once you've written the content, the final, critical step is promoting it. There are three steps to a complete promotional strategy, and between each of these you'll create a balanced, sustainable flow of traffic to each article.

Step One: Promote To Your Audience
This is the fastest, easiest part of the promotional strategy. If you have an audience already, you just need to let them know that this new piece of content is ready for them to check out. Your audience has already opted in to hear from you, whether that was by following you on social media or subscribing to your email list or podcast, and because of that you know where to find them. Go ahead and add the article to each of the social platforms you're on, add it to

any recurring social media scheduling you have running, and send it to your email list as well. If you're part of any relevant groups online, including private Facebook groups, message boards and forums, put it up there as well. Share it via your personal networks, too, including your personal Facebook, Twitter and LinkedIn accounts.

Step Two: Promote To Other Audiences
Promoting to other audiences is where you can get those sudden surges of traffic that can help an article rank quickly.

Reddit is a great platform for this, if you can target it correctly. Identify a sub-reddit where the content would be relevant and post it there. The easiest way to get started is to find the communities that let you drop in a link as a stand-alone submission. Others will require you to start a discussion, in which case you should give some context to the piece, share some free resources and generally make it valuable and appealing. Reddit users will flay you if you come across as self-promotional, so make sure you take a really generous approach without asking anything in return. Don't make them opt in — just let them have it. You can always use a retargeting pixel if you're desperate to capture the traffic immediately.

You can email it to influencers who are mentioned in the piece, or who you think would enjoy it. *Don't ask them to share it* — it's not their job to promote your stuff. Just let them know you think they might get a kick out of it. If they really like it and think it's valuable, they might share it, and you've created a good connection without draining any goodwill at the outset.

Step Three: Adding To Your Structure

This is the most overlooked part of SEO strategy. If an article is going to perform well in search, it needs to be as valuable in three years as it is today. In order for it to continue being useful, people who are arriving to your site fresh need to be able to find it, along with older content and more recent content. As you are writing and publishing content, then, you need to be creating overarching themes that all the content falls under. You want to be linking to past articles that are related, as well as having specific pages that collect themes on your site. For example, you might have a page on your site that lists all the articles you've written about improving operations in business. Each of those articles should link back to this index page, and the index page should link to each of the articles. This way, anyone can find all your content on a particular topic, and it's a powerful way to link all the related content on your site together rather than having each article in an individual silo. Using this strategy means that when one article ranks well, it gradually improves the ranking of all the articles it is linked to.

Update old articles to link to new ones. Add notes to the older articles that direct readers to read more content on your site, and boost the performance of the newer articles by trading off the power of the older ones. Make sure that if you come back to a particular topic in your new content, that you link back to the older pieces to create a 'web of knowledge' on your site, rather than having just a chronological sequence of updates.

Finally... You Wait.

SEO is a long-term strategy. Once you've created the content and promoted it, you just have to wait and see. It doesn't take very much to get an article on Google's radar — often a few hundred visits is enough to get it noticed — but it could take three months or more to get it consistently ranked. This is where people come unstuck. They're frustrated and worried that they're not ranking yet, so they start finding lots of little hacks that will supposedly improve their performance, but often end up undoing all their hard work. When you get to this point, just chill. You have to be patient, so instead of fretting and fiddling, repeat this process so that you're using the lag time effectively and setting yourself up for repeated SEO success.

Action Steps for Chapter Nine:

1. Make a list of the existing topics and new topics you could create content for.
2. Do keyword research for 20-30 keywords within those topics:
   a. Research the addressable keywords
   b. Assess the keyword volume
   c. Assess the competition
   d. Choose your keywords
   e. Add your chosen keywords to your Quarterly Content Planner
3. Go back through your existing content and perform an audit on the SEO. Build out the structure of older posts, interlinking your content, so that all the posts help each other increase in performance.

Chapter Ten: Honing Your Conversion Potential

The powerful thing about content marketing is that your assets increase in value over time. Whether it's your blog or your book, as you continue to add to the content and distribute it to expanding market segments, you'll see greater and greater returns on your earlier investments. That said, your content can always be better. Whether you make your new content premium from the outset, or if you go back and periodically update it, you can always be adding more value to your market and improving your reputation and authority as a result.

As your offering and messaging clarify over time, you'll probably want to make your content gradually more sophisticated, and this will happen in tandem with your audience becoming more sophisticated, which we'll talk about later in this chapter. But first, we need to talk about *Influence*.

Understanding The Six Principles of Influence

If you could only choose one book to read about sales and marketing, Dr Robert Cialdini's *Influence: The Psychology of Persuasion* should be it. His 'Six Principles of Influence' will shape your understanding about your customers and your market more than any number of other books could possibly do. Just about every piece of persuasive content you've ever consumed will be based around these principles.

Cialdini's book was originally published in 1984, but has continued in print uninterrupted since then. It is so powerful, and so popular, because it cuts to the core of what drives people to act. When a revised copy of the book was republished in 2001, Cialdini wrote a piece for the Harvard Business Review, capturing the essence of its power in a single stroke:

"Persuasion is governed by several principles that can be taught and applied... By mastering these principles–and, the author stresses, using them judiciously and ethically–executives can learn the elusive art of capturing an audience, swaying the undecided, and converting the opposition."

Now, before we jump in, let's expand on 'judicious use': These principles can be used for good, or for evil. If you are planning on the latter, stop that. There's enough evil in the world without marketers contributing to it and making things worse for everyone. But if you're here to serve your customers and do the best you can for them, read on. By recognizing certain behaviors and using these principles in a positive way, we can capture a market, persuade prospects, and drive purchases.

Principle One: Reciprocity
You've heard it a million times:

"You scratch my back and I'll scratch yours."

Reciprocity is based on goodwill debt. When someone does you a favor, it triggers a psychological indebtedness, a desire to "even the score". From an evolutionary viewpoint, humans are hardwired to return the favor to maintain social equilibrium. That means that when someone offers us their time, money, or effort, we feel like we owe them until we've given them something of similar value — and only then are we even. When it comes to persuading your customers, then, "you have to go first," Cialdini urges.

"Give something: give information, give free samples, give a positive experience to people and they will want to give you something in return."

There are many things you can give potential customers. It could be a sample, a risk-free trial, free shipping, free training, or some other gift. These offerings create reciprocity. They make your customer feel like they owe you, which makes them more likely to respond positively to your future requests.

Principle Two: Consistency and Commitment

Most people are constantly updating their tastes, preferences and opinions. But most of us also feel obligated to act consistently in public. To stay consistent, we make new decisions that align with past actions and speech. This is to avoid cognitive dissonance (the mental discomfort that comes from doing something inconsistent with our self-perception.)

This is why the 'yes ladder' technique works in sales. You get your potential customer to say yes to something small:

"It's a nice day, isn't it?"

Once they say yes to that, you ask them another question that's more related to your point. You lead them through several of these questions, positioning each one to get a 'yes' response, until you get to your offer. By that stage, they've said yes so many times that it's uncomfortable and incongruent for them to say no.

Principle Three: Social Proof

Aristotle said:

"Man is by nature a social animal."

Humans observe the actions of other humans so they can make better decisions. Where do you turn when you're planning a trip to a place you've never been? TripAdvisor. How do you determine if a new movie is worth watching? Check IMDB or Rotten Tomatoes. Aristotle wasn't around long enough to witness today's 'review culture', and it didn't exist when Cialdini wrote his book in 1984. But social proof is an immutable principle. We depend on input from others for both important and mundane decisions. A large part of this is about risk mitigation: if it's working well for everyone else, then it should work for me, right?

Think about the last time you checked out a company, and found they had no reviews or social media presence. Unless you were referred by someone you trust, you probably decided to take your business elsewhere. Referrals and testimonials prove to potential customers that they're in good company before they buy. No one wants to be the fool that took a risk on you and lost. Showcase the community that supports you and your company to make your business more appealing to prospects.

Principle Four: Authority

Humans experience a wide range of psychological fallacies, but one of the more powerful is the 'appeal to authority'. This is when an authority figure is invoked as proof that something is true or desirable. This is why endorsements from experts or celebrities can blow up conversions and sales.

(Authority is trustworthy, so if you can manage it, get an authority figure to endorse your brand. The authority factor take the principle of social proof to a whole new level. Get a testimonial from a notable person or business in your niche and get it in front of your prospects.)

The appeal to authority works in content because it leverages what's known as referent power. When you refer to *someone else* who has power, you get a halo effect.[7] Your reader thinks of you as being in the same circle as that authority figure, and so they also perceive you as being just as influential and trustworthy.

Principle Five: Liking

It might seem silly… but how much your prospects like you has a major impact on whether they'll buy from you. Humans are tribal creatures — we prioritize people in our close circles over strangers all the time. We get into close circles by being likeable and trustworthy, so you need to work out how to communicate that about yourself to your customers. If they like you, they'll cooperate with your requests. And people like *other* people who share their interests, values, and personality traits. Sure, you're probably not going to be besties with your customers, but it's actually not too hard to manufacture a sense of 'sameness' with your customers.

Most people think of businesses as impersonal entities. That's why it's key that your business seem friendly as soon as the customer encounters you. Make

---

[7] See French and Raven's 'Bases of Social Power' for more on the types of power and how they can be used in a range of situations:
(http://web.mit.edu/curhan/www/docs/Articles/15341_Readings/Power/French_&_Raven_Studies_Social_Power_ch9_pp150-167.pdf)

sure you have an attractive, functional website. Other things to focus on include…

- Speaking the language of your target market (keeping your copy consistent and appealing, using the same vocabulary and linguistic patterns as your customers to communicate "I'm just like you")
- Surprising the prospect with unexpected messages or cool giveaways. This demonstrates high value, and helps you to build that goodwill balance
- Overdelivering with bonuses or upgrades to create little dopamine hits for the customer (which in turn makes them feel good every time they think about you)

Principle Six: Scarcity

The consumer market today seems to live in a chronic state of FOMO (fear of missing out). People hate missing out on deals. It's why "limited time only" and "last in stock" offers work so well. Customers will often buy impulsively if they're scared of missing out.

It's why airlines tell you how many seats are left on the flight you're looking at, and why restaurants always tell you they only have two tables left when you call to book. Rarity always increases a product's perceived value.

It's why luxury cars, precious jewels and limited release albums always sell out. People want what others can't have, and so scarcity signals almost always increase sales. You can use countdown timers and stock counter to show customers that they're at risk of missing out. Make sure the pressure is real — people work it out fast when you try to manufacture scarcity, and will call you out for it — but don't underestimate the value of triggering FOMO and urgency in your customers. It's a powerful motivation and has made many fortunes.

• • •

The power of Cialdini's Six Principles lies in their simple appeals to human nature. Use them in combination, and deploy them throughout your marketing. They can transform your customer acquisition and your business as a result. Again, remember that people are perceptive — your customers are not idiots. In fact, they're probably smarter than you, and they deserve your respect. Don't be dodgy, and don't try to sell them stuff that doesn't work.

The key is to keep their interests at heart and serve them better than anyone else can or will. Be honest and real with your customers, and you'll get their loyalty. It's the foundation of long-term success, and the most valuable thing you can earn.

Understanding and Leveraging Market Sophistication

Every market has varying levels of sophistication. How much does your audience know about the kind of offer you are making? Do they need a lot of education, or do they know all the details already? This is a critical concept covered originally by Eugene Schwartz, in his unbeatable book, *Breakthrough Advertising* (which, despite being listed on Amazon at $275 at the time of writing — and sometimes as much as $1000 — is worth every cent and will make you your money back quickly. This is strongly recommended reading for increasing your understanding of how markets adapt and behave).

Markets who have never heard about an offering like yours need very different messaging to markets who know the offering intimately. For example, if you're selling espresso machines to Italian restaurants, your market is probably very sophisticated. If you're selling cloud accounting software to middle-aged bookkeepers, your market is probably quite unsophisticated. You need to know where your customers lie on this spectrum.

Schwartz believed that there were five levels of market sophistication in all:

Stage One: Completely Unsophisticated

You're first to market with a new product or service. Your prospects have never seen anything like your offering, and so they're easily impressed, likely to believe what you tell them, and open to buying without too much hard selling. If you find yourself in this position — and it happens more frequently than you might think — keep your copy simple. Focus on the need your product addresses, or on the big claim you want to become known for. Again, keep it simple. No need to complicate with long explanations. Just focus on what the customer will get out of using your product.

Example: "Lose Your Love Handles!"

Stage Two: Somewhat Sophisticated

If you're among the first few providers in your market, your prospects have likely progressed to the second stage of sophistication. They are aware that they have a problem and that a solution exists, they're still excited by the claims being made about this kind of product, but they're beginning to be a bit more discerning. So at this stage, you want to stick with the single claim, but push it to the limit. Add some details that make your offer irresistible, and that your competitors can't beat you on. Over time, you have to make bigger and better claims, until you reach the cap of what the market will accept.

Example: "Get Back in Your Skinny Jeans In Two Weeks, or Your Money Back" or "Lose 20 Pounds or We'll Pay YOU!"

Stage Three: Sophistication

At this stage, your market has heard all the claims. You and your competitors have been going at it tooth and nail to make the best offer, and people are getting a little jaded by it all. At this stage, you need to differentiate yourself from the rest of your industry: the problem people want to solve still exists; new and repeat buyers are emerging, but prospects are more skeptical and have more information available to them. The way to get their attention anew is to show them *how* your product works — what Schwartz called a 'new mechanism'. This is a fresh way of presenting an existing solution, in a way that reengages the prospect by piquing their curiosity.

Example: "Blocks the Part of Your Brain That Makes You Hungry" or "Added Fiber Makes You Feel Fuller for Longer!"

Stage Four: Saturated Sophistication

Usually, Stage Three sophistication only lasts a few months to a year. The market is moving too quickly for any one claim to sustain the level of sales needed to keep each business going. At this stage, you need to go back to the elaboration strategy used in Stage Two. You need to expand on *why* the mechanism works and go into greater detail about why this solution is so effective. It needs to demonstrate how your product solves a greater range of problems, creates extra benefits and works more effectively than ever before.

Example: "Wonder Drug Blocks Hunger Hormone to Reduce Cravings and Increase Satiety After Meals"

Stage Five: Skeptical Sophistication

It usually takes a long time for markets to reach this level of sophistication. At this stage, they are completely tapped out. They've heard every claim under the sun, and they don't care to hear another one ever again. (This is the stage that the tobacco industry has reached — no one would believe them if they advertised cigarettes as increasing your social status or good for your health. The only way for tobacco companies to get ahead is to position cigarettes in films, music videos and art. Positioning cigarettes as 'cool' or associated with an aspirational lifestyle is their only play now.) If your market reaches this stage, or if you're in Stage Four and are reaching the limit of claims you can make, here's what you do: appeal to your prospect's sense of identity, and to their intrinsic motivations. Do they want to be seen as successful? Beautiful? Clever? A leader in their field? Associate your product with people who have achieved those outcomes and invite the prospect to join their exclusive ranks.

Example: "The Most Desirable Women In The World Wear [Scent]"

Action Steps for Chapter Ten:

1. Work through each of Cialdini's Six Principles. How can you put each of them to use in your content?

2. Assess your market's sophistication:

   a. What is the messaging being used in your competitor's marketing?

   b. What are the questions customers are asking you?

   c. How can you take advantage of the current level of sophistication (and how you can prepare for the next stage)?

Chapter Eleven: Writing Copy

"Copywriting is salesmanship in print." — *Gary Halbert*

Good copywriting can generate millions of dollars for your business. So while it's only one element of your content marketing strategy (and the final element to be developed), it's an incredibly important one. Copywriting is critical to the success of your business, because it allows you to persuade customers to take a specific action, and to pay you in the process. To get people to take that kind of action, you need to understand psychology and persuasion, and you need to be willing to put in the time to build a deep, visceral understanding of how each of those elements fit together in your specific business.

The best copywriters spend *years* honing their skills. They study sales, psychology, advertising and market trends to develop a strong, intuitive level of what gets customers to act. It's a whole career — you can't just add 'write sales page' onto the end of your to-do list and expect the resulting copy to perform. I can't emphasize how critical this is: you could have the best product or service in the market, but if your copy sucks, all the work you've done up to this point will be for nothing. And it *will* suck if you don't take the time to learn and hone your copywriting abilities.

Derek Johanson, creator of the CopyHour.com copywriting course, looks at it like this:

"Most of the time, businesses are going to do much better by hiring out the production of their sales letters and other copywriting tasks to a professional. If you are the business owner, spending all this time trying to write sales pages or

funnels is a waste — you would be better off focusing on the things in your business that you're actually good at. You can get high quality work without spending a fortune, and a professional will do a much better job than you will.

You can tell when business owners have written the copy, because they make all kinds of mistakes: they don't understand the medium they're writing for, they use language that's totally wrong, and they don't address the market effectively. To have great copy that converts well, you need to understand what has been promised to this market in the past, which of those promises have been fulfilled, and which have not. This allows you to find the gap where your business has the most opportunity, so you can emphasize what sets you apart from your competitors and why customers will benefit so much from working with you."

Someone who understands the business you're in, who can get to the core of your market's wants and needs, and who can weave an offer together seamlessly — that's the person you want writing your funnels and sales pages. Yes, a good copywriter will charge you more than it would cost to do it yourself — but they'll also *make* you far more money with their copy than you would make if you wrote it yourself. Some copywriters work for flat fees, others take a revenue or profit share, others still ask for a combination. But if they are a proven professional, and you're serious about selling your product or service to the top end of the market, find the money they're asking for. You'll make it back in spades.

If working with someone else just isn't on the cards, then there are the five principles for you to understand before you ever write a word. Once you've worked through these, we'll look at how to structure your sales copy and three copywriting formulas you can use to make sure that your copy performs as well as possible.

Copywriting Principles

Principle One: Define Your Audience and Tailor Your Message Accordingly

I know, I know, we've been through this, but it bears restating: Your copy should speak to a very clearly defined market segment and no one else. Your copy should simultaneously repel people who are not in that segment — and you can be very specific about this. It's often easier to start by defining who your business is *not* for and then honing in on your ideal audience once you've got rid of the distractions.

Here's an example from the About page from Frank Kern's website, one of the giants of internet marketing:

"I can <u>not</u> help you get rich quick… If you don't want to advertise, you're not going to enjoy my stuff… If you're looking for the easy way, I don't want to help you. It's important you understand what I'm telling you. I can help you, I just won't. I'm capable of it, but I refuse to do it."
(See www.frankkern.com/about)

Through the rest of the content on that page, Kern goes on to let you know that he wants to work with small business owners who really care about their customers, who are committed to doing the hard work necessary to succeed, and to people who are willing to try out his suggestions, in exchange for him being able to make them sales offers. Another great example of this is Eben Pagan's 'Get Altitude' business training programs (see www.getaltitude.com). As soon as you land on the page, you're asked to make a choice: do you want to start a business online, grow your business systems, or get more customers? Every visitor to that site is immediately segmented by their interest and will receive tailored marketing that speaks directly to that interest.

Principle Two: Address Their Problem

Every prospect you will ever deal with have some issue they are looking for help to solve, and this is where you want to go deep. You want to address the one specific thing that you can help them solve, demonstrating a deep understanding of their struggle. The goal is to be able to describe their needs better than they can, and to demonstrate empathy, understanding and authority. When you know their situation better than they do, you're the one they'll turn to when they're ready to act.

Some copywriting advice out there tells you to twist the knife, to really try to aggravate the issue they're facing, but in my view it's better to explore the problem with them, to let them know that you're on their side and understand what they're going through. Your copy should be a bridge for them, not a wrecking ball that crushes them. You want to describe the situation in a way that makes them think *"Exactly. Finally, someone who gets it."*

Principle Three: Explain Why Their Current Approach Isn't Solving The Problem

Robert Collier, a master salesman, said that you have to "…enter the conversation in your prospect's head." It's your job to get inside their thought patterns, anticipating their questions and objections. You want to think of every reason someone might bring up to avoid converting on your offer — *we don't have the money for this, I need to speak to my business partner, we're already doing too much* — and address it head on before they talk themselves out of taking you up on your offer. And make no mistake: people *will* talk themselves out of things if given the chance, so you have to make sure you beat the little voice in their head to the punch.

This is also your opportunity to address all your competitors solutions and to point out why they a) won't work and b) yours is better. Remember: this is <u>not</u> an opportunity to talk smack about other people in your industry. It's a chance to differentiate yourself in a positive way and highlight why customers would be better served working with you, by showing that you have a deep, intrinsic understanding of their needs and perspective.

<u>Principle Four: Demonstrate How Your Offering WILL Solve The Problem</u>

This is where you define their problem around your solution, so that what you're offering seems like a natural fit for them. At this point, you show them that it would be much too painful/costly/time-consuming/difficult for them to develop this kind of solution on their own, but that you've made the whole thing *really* easy for them, and that they'll get results *much* faster than they ever could on their own.

You want to paint a picture of how their future will be different as a result of taking you up on your offer, and to showcase your credibility in a way that stops people in their tracks. Outline the specific benefits they'll experience as a result of your work — whether it's more revenue, less churn, more efficient systems, greater throughput, or whatever — and use lots of testimonials to back yourself up. Let your reader know that lots of other people like them have changed their whole situation by working with you.

Principle Five: Make The Offer

This is the final, critical step — *make the offer.* Invite them to purchase your product or service. Explain why you're charging this amount, and what kind of risk mitigation you're offering (guarantees are powerful and go far beyond 'money back' — you can guarantees the quality of work, customer grace period, bonuses, unlimited support or revisions, additional features, free replacements etc). It's at this point that you also want to add a little urgency or scarcity (if you can actually create them, not if they're faked), and let them know what will happen if they don't act. Restate your offer, and tell them specifically what next steps they need to take to get this great offer.

Learning these principles, and working out how to apply them to your particular offer might sound like a lot of work... and it is. When you consider that one of the greatest ways of learning copywriting is to write out the greatest ads of all time *by hand*, you might feel a little overwhelmed. After all — how are you meant to find all these pieces of copy? How are you meant to know if you're making progress as you're working through them?

This is a problem many copywriters have had since Gary "Prince Of Print" Halbert recommended it to his proteges. And it was a problem that frustrated Derek Johanson so much that he created CopyHour. CopyHour is a systematic way to learn copy at a deep level, embedding the principles of persuasive print and presentation in your brain in 60 minutes per day. All you have to do is show up and write. Over time, if you commit to the process and do the work, you'll become better than 99% of all the copywriters out there. You'll get a deep understanding of what makes copy work, and what makes it flop. I've been through the course twice myself, and most of the successful copywriters I know have done it too — if you're going to write copy, there's no excuse for not doing CopyHour. (I'm not getting any kind of commission for saying that, either. Handwriting successful ads is really the only way to learn.)

Copywriting Formulas

Once you've deeply ingrained the principles of copywriting there are a few formulas you can use to make sure you hit on all the key elements. You should note that any successful content that is created in your business — whether it's blog content, email funnels, customer communications or social media content — is based on concepts of persuasive copywriting, and so these formulas work for other formats too.

While there are many, many formulas you can use, I just recommend three. Let me remind you that *research* is the most important element of any successful piece of copy, so before you start, make sure you know exactly who the copy is for and what kind of conversation is going on in their head. Make sure you know the history of the market, what has and has not been delivered, and what the level of market sophistication is (like we discussed in the last chapter). Make sure you're familiar with your competition and what they're offering, as well as being able to highlight your specific points of difference.

Formula One: AIDA

Maybe the most commonly discussed of the copywriting formulas, AIDA stands for Attention, Interest, Desire, Action. This formula is specific enough to help you include some key elements, but not so specific that is becomes prescriptive. It leads with *attention*, which is critical currency in copywriting — if you don't get your reader's attention, and keep it, there's no way you're making a sale. Your headline is the key attention-grabbing device. Remember that comment earlier in the book from advertising legend David Ogilvy? Here's a refresher:

"On the average, five times as many people read the headline as read the body copy. When you have written your headline, you have spent eighty cents out of your dollar."

Your headline needs to stop your reader dead in their tracks. It has to reach out and grab their attention, to interrupt their scroll through Facebook or to get them to click a link in an email. Once you have their attention, you need to hold their *interest*. This is where you address their problem and "join in the conversation in their head". Let them know that you get it, and that you're going to help them solve it.

Now that you've got them interested, it's time to stimulate their *desire* for your solution. Paint a picture of what they can expect from working with you — testimonials and case studies are great resources to include to do this. Show that your solution has worked for other people just like your reader, and that it's a safe bet for them to go ahead with you. Finally, invite them to take *action*. Never leave it to them to work it out themselves: tell them exactly what they need to do next to get what you're offering. Tell them how much it's going to cost, mitigate any risk they might be seeing and drive them to take the action.

Formula Two: FAB

This is a nice simple formula that works well across a range of verticals, and translates well to other types of content as well (like blog posts, social media posts and so on). Highlighting the Features, Advantages and Benefits of your product or service is pretty straightforward, and allows you to map out your copy in a more technical style than the other two formulas listed here.

This is a great option when there's not a pressing problem that your offer solves. If it's a non-essential or 'nice to have', then FAB is probably the best way to structure your copy. In this method, you outline all the *features* of your offer: the technical or factual details about it. This is the stuff that no one can argue with: the structure of your deals, the materials you use or your production process. After each feature, you want to add why that feature is an *advantage* (how it sets the customer apart from the market, or how it solves a problem), and then what the *benefit* of that feature is (the outcomes they can expect to see as a result of the feature and it's unique advantages).

Formula Three: A FOREST

This one is a little longer than AIDA and FAB, but if you have a very high price-point offer, this is probably the option you want to go with. It's ideal for long-form sales copy (such as multi-thousand word sales pages), because it gets the reader into a rhythm and uses linguistic patterns that helps them to receive your message. Let's break it down.

A: Alliteration — Also known as 'head rhyme', alliteration gets readers in really receptive rhythm.

F: Facts — You can't argue with facts. Facts help people buy into your argument.

O: Opinions — Opinions that jive with those of your reader are likely to generate an emotional commitment from them: they create confirmation bias.

R: Repetition — Saying the same thing a few different ways makes sure that every reader 'gets it'. People need to hear the message in the way that makes the most sense to them.

E: Examples — Illustrate your point with tangible examples that your reader can relate to or imagine themselves experiencing.

S: Statistics — These add credibility to your argument. Make sure they're correct, but once confirmed, use liberally. See the points on Facts.

T: Threes — Repeat something three times to make it memorable. Like alliteration, threes create a special rhythm in the brain that tends to help information 'stick'.

◆ ◆ ◆

Alternately, you can skip the neat formulas and take a much more detailed approach, which is something Johanson recommends particularly when creating long pieces of sales copy. You'll see that elements of Cialdini's Six Principles are laced throughout this method, which is why it's so effective.

Part One: The Lead

This is your introduction. You can either start with a pattern-interrupt to get their attention, or go straight to the headline. Once that's in place, fill out the rest of the lead. This is where you address yourself to the specific customer persona, introduce the problem or concept, and if you're feeling ready, build some scarcity into what you're about to share.

Part Two: The Sales Argument

If it's appropriate for your particular business, you can transition into your creation story here. This is where you differentiate yourself from the market, and establish some likeability and authority, by sharing how and why your business got started, and what you've gone on to achieve. Once this is built out, you enter into your sales argument. You outline the myths and misconceptions around the problem you're solving, or you emphasize how urgent an opportunity this offer is for the reader.

Part Three: The Offer

Once you've built up some tension around the problem, you can outline the features of your product and their benefits in bullet points to create a strong visual emphasis. Every time you make a specific claim, include a testimonial that provides hard proof that your claim is accurate.

Part Four: The Close

We've talked about how important it is to *make the offer*, and this is the moment. If appropriate, you can use a 'false close' if you want — letting the reader know that they'll get some special bonuses if they go ahead right now — but otherwise, it's time to make the price presentation. Before you reveal the number, position your offer as the best fit for the reader's problem, the reasons *why* it's the best fit, how it's different from the market and so on…and then reveal the price. Once it's out there, you can outline the ordering details and guarantees. Restate the price and list any options you might have about how they can get it (such as payment plans or group buys), and then close out with FAQs if that's the right fit for you.

Action Steps for Chapter Eleven:

1. Create a list of bullet point responses to each of the five copywriting principles, to see how you're currently using them in your sales copy, and how they could be improved.
2. Create an outline for a sales page, using each of the three formulas to create three separate outlines. Make a list of all the information that would need to go into each of the outlines in order to really capture your readers and make them want to convert.
3. Map out what it would take to overhaul all your existing copy to reflect these principle and formulas, and decide whether you're going to handle this yourself or work with an established copywriter.

Chapter Twelve: The Round-Up

There are five key things you should take away from this book. These are the underpinning principles of my approach to content marketing, and if you absorb nothing else, these will stand you in good stead.

1. Your content should give away the farm.

If you've spent any amount of time reading business content online, you'll know that anything you produce should "add value." In fact, you've probably seen that phrase so many times you want to throw your computer out the window. It's a vague, useless platitude that has lost all it's meaning, so let me be clear:

Your content should tell your readers (be they customer or competitor) exactly how you do business. It should tell them how they can do it the exact same way. This book is an example of this principle in action — the content you've just worked through is everything I do for my clients, from blogging to ghostwriting to copywriting. I have not kept back any secrets or key elements of my process, and yours should give away the same amount of detail.

Many business owners are resistant to this, since it feels risky. Maybe your competitors will steal your ideas, or maybe your customers will just go and do it themselves... but for the most part, they won't. Inertia is a powerful force, and it stops people from implementing anything that's new or difficult or complex. The upside, of course, is that by sharing all your expertise and insight, you become the go-to authority on the topic. Whenever someone has a problem you've talked about, you're the only business they're going to think about — no one else has made plain how they would handle it. Do not underestimate how much people hate having to deal with something they're not interested in. Putting your content out there with total transparency inspires confidence and trust in prospects to know that you get exactly what they need, and can handle it for them smoothly, letting them get on with the things they're good at and like doing.

2. Forget about tactics. You need strategy and systems.

Like I said above, so much content in the marketing space is focused around "adding value". Unfortunately, to keep turning out such a high volume, creators have turned to publishing very low-level tactical information that does little to move your business forward in any meaningful way. Yes, split-testing the colors of your buy buttons can yield a lift in conversions. Yes, optimizing all your title tags can bump you up the search rankings. But does it create long-term momentum in your business? No.

It's critical that any marketing you implement has a clear, overarching strategy directing it. Think of this as the North Star for your business, against which every decision is measured. For example, the intent behind your marketing might be to establish you as the authority leader in your industry, positioned to work with the top end of the market. Every decision you make, then, can be held up against this metric: Will publishing that in-depth blog post get you closer to that goal? Yes, so go ahead. Will fiddling around with button colors help you get there? No, so don't bother.

Once your strategy is in place, you need a simple system that allows you to capitalize on the momentum created by your content. For example, your system might look like this:

Blog post or book > opt-in offer > email onboarding sequence + call to action > sales offer > further segmentation.

Your system does not need to be highly complex: it simply needs to drive prospects towards the action you want them to take (which should in turn move your business closer to your North Star). Keep it simple and strategic.

3. Your content is your ambassador.

Most of your prospects will have their first interaction with your brand via your content. Whether it's a blog post, a podcast, a video, a social media update or a sales letter, that piece of content is going to form their first impression of you — and we all know you don't get a second chance at those.

Every piece of content that is published under your brand should be the best possible representation of who you are. It should be polished and accurate, appealing and trustworthy — it should be *good*. If you can't make it good yourself, hire someone who can.

Don't publish incorrect information, don't bad-mouth your competitors, and don't talk down to your audience. Take the time to find out who your audience is and how they communicate, and tailor your content accordingly. Use it to get inside the conversation going on inside their head, and to invite them to share that conversation with you.

4. Content is not a refuge from sales.

It's easy to feel highly productive when you're focusing on content marketing. You can produce a blog post every day and people on the internet will tell you you're *amaaazing...* but amazing does not put dollars in the bank. People who claim to make money from no-sell content marketing are either flukes or liars, and neither is a good option if you plan to grow a sustainable business.

I've said it several times throughout this book, but once more for the record: you *must* make sales offers for your content marketing strategy to be successful. You *must* position your content in such a way that it's natural to offer prospects a purchasing opportunity and for them to take you up on it.

Content is not a silver bullet. It requires a lot of hard work, and it does take time to start paying off. But it will pay off if you use it properly and not as a crutch to avoid doing other, more uncomfortable things in your business.

5. Recognize when you're not the best person to create the content.

Most business owners are very territorial about letting other people anywhere near customer-facing content. It's understandable — if you've spent years building a business, honing your expertise and establishing your credibility, you want to keep a tight handle on everything. Unfortunately, that's usually a terrible idea. As your business grows, you have more and more things you have to handle, and content is a time-consuming strategy. It requires a lot of attention and tweaking, and you can easily spend whole days getting a particular piece right... and that's assuming you're *good* at content.

Many entrepreneurs and businesspeople would rather do anything else than create content. You might be one of them — maybe you don't feel like you're a strong writer, or you just know that it takes you ages to get anything out.

Maybe you have millions of ideas and no idea how to start communicating them. Maybe you have an incredible offering but haven't been able to communicate it in a way that gets attention and sales from the right people.

Whichever camp you fall into, finding a content partner for your business can create very powerful leverage. Working with someone who has proven expertise in content creation and copywriting will pay off in spades, both making you money and freeing up your time and resources.

To that end, if you'd like to explore working together on your content marketing strategy or copywriting, I'd like to invite you to contact me at laura@laurahanly.com. Yes, I'm making you an offer.

My agency handles three things: recurring monthly blog content and all the funnels that go with it; ghostwriting books that position you as the expert in your industry; and copywriting sales materials. I take on a limited number of clients each quarter to guarantee exceptional service, and I only work with businesses who are committed to providing the best quality content to their customers, and who understand the standards required to get those conversions. If that's you, then please reach out to me, either at laura@laurahanly.com, or through my website, www.laurahanly.com.

• • •

Thank you for reading Content That Converts. It's been a privilege to have been able to share it with you. I hope you'll use it to create a system that consistently brings customers into your business and turns them into lifelong relationships. If you know other business owners who would benefit from reading this, please let me know at the email address above, and I'll be in touch to send them a copy directly.

Finally, if you'd like to join a growing group of world-class marketers and entrepreneurs talking about content marketing strategy across a range of businesses, you can join the Content That Converts Facebook group at facebook.com/groups/ContentThatConverts/. You'll find plenty of bonus content in there, including the process I used to write this book, the research I'm doing on marketing strategy and much more. I'm looking forward to getting to know you and helping you grow your business with Content That Converts.

Acknowledgements

My deep, deep gratitudes go out to Rob Hanly, Ruth Gale, Nat Eliason, Derek Johanson, Rachel Mazza, Laura Hietala, Alexis Shields and Kimberly Rich for all the support, feedback and resources you've given me to make this book happen. All the members of the Content That Converts Facebook group are also deeply appreciated — your feedback on the outline, the title and the cover were so helpful.

I'd also like to mention the people who, directly or indirectly, pushed me to write a book of my own, and have helped me make it a success out in the world: Taylor Pearson, Lindsay Marder, Molly Pittman, Tim Conley and Ben Krueger. You guys made me see what was possible (and right in front of me).

Finally, thanks again to you. There's a lot of marketing content out there and it's humbling (and really, really exciting) that you've chosen mine. If you've got questions or need direction on something in your content marketing, join the Facebook group (facebook.com/groups/ContentThatConverts/) or hit me up on Twitter: I'm @lauhanly, and I'll get back to you as soon as I can.

Made in the USA
San Bernardino, CA
28 December 2016